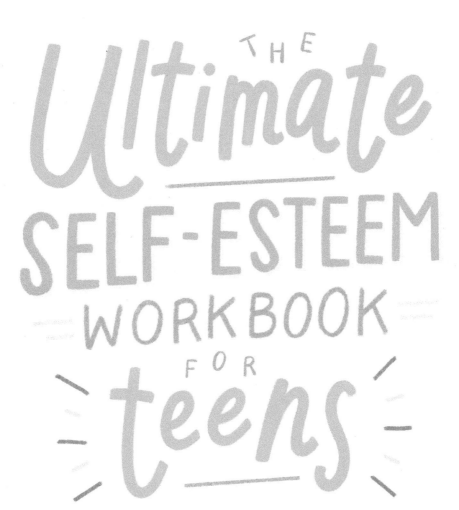

THE Ultimate SELF-ESTEEM WORKBOOK FOR teens

OVERCOME INSECURITY, DEFEAT YOUR INNER CRITIC, AND LIVE CONFIDENTLY

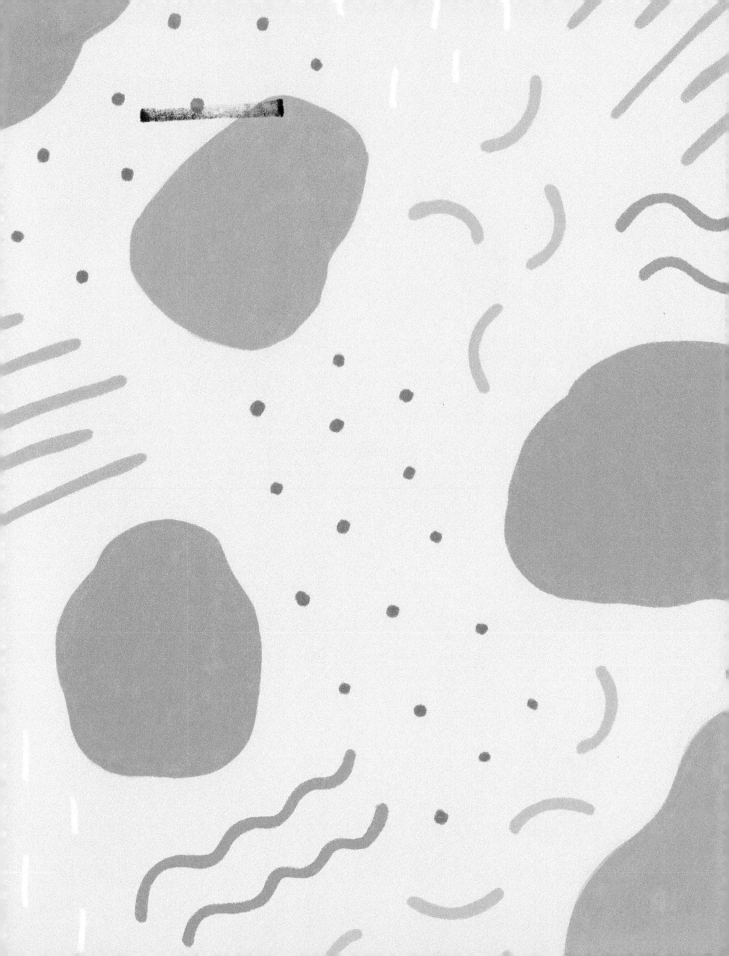

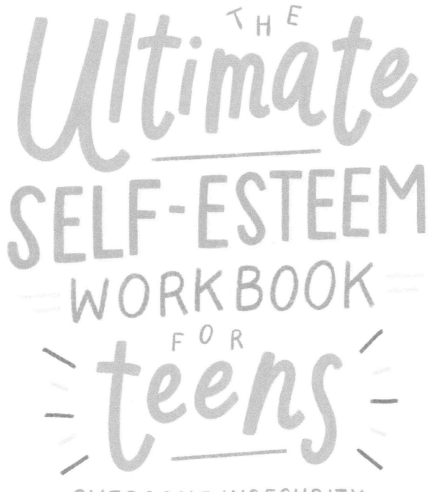

THE Ultimate SELF-ESTEEM WORKBOOK FOR teens

OVERCOME INSECURITY, DEFEAT YOUR INNER CRITIC, AND LIVE CONFIDENTLY

Megan MacCutcheon, LPC

Illustrations by Rhianna Marie Chan

ROCKRIDGE PRESS

Interior Designer: Stephanie Sumulong
Art Manager: Janice Ackerman
Editor: Lia Ottaviano
Production Editor: Kurt Shulenberger
Cover Design and Illustrations: Rhianna Marie Chan

ISBN: Print 978-1-64152-610-4 | eBook 978-1-64152-611-1

To my kids:
Knowing the chaos and confusion of adolescence,
I often fear the time when you will become teens.
I hope you each forge your own path with
self-confidence, good judgment, and the knowledge
that you are worthy and so very loved.

CONTENTS

INTRODUCTION

Hi! Welcome to *The Ultimate Self-Esteem Workbook for Teens.* You may have picked up this book on your own, hoping to find ways to feel better. Or maybe your school counselor or therapist recommended it to you. Perhaps you were bribed by a parent to read it. Regardless of how this book found its way into your hands, I'm really glad you're giving it a shot!

My name is Megan and I'm a therapist who has focused much of my work on helping people improve their self-esteem. I especially love working with teenagers, who, just like you (and practically every other teenager on the planet!), could use a little help improving their confidence and navigating the confusion and overwhelming stress of adolescence.

It may feel like you're alone, struggling with things like insecurity, depression, or anxiety. But you definitely aren't: There are lots of other people of all ages out there facing many of the same issues. So many people deal with self-esteem issues, regardless of age, or how they might look, act, and present themselves to the outside world. This may be hard to believe, but it's true. There are tons of different ways to mask or hide self-esteem struggles, but so many people have them. We just don't often talk about them!

The reality is, almost everyone I've worked with in my practice (and that's hundreds of people) have faced some type of self-esteem issue, regardless of the original reason they decided to meet with me. I've found that insecurity and low levels of self-esteem are at the root of many other issues like stress, depression, anxiety, and relationship problems. People don't always think they have a self-esteem problem. But when we dig deeper into the issues they're facing, we often find that improving self-esteem will be one of the keys to help them feel better and live more rewarding lives.

You may have been really pissed off, rolled your eyes, or wanted to scream if you were gifted this book by somebody else, but bear with me. Whether you are feeling depressed, confused, or completely alone, you don't have to feel that way forever. Maybe you're dealing with changing friend groups, figuring out your identity, navigating the complicated world of sexuality and dating, or learning how to get along with your family as you mature. You might be struggling with how to conduct yourself at parties where there are drugs and alcohol. Or you may feel completely stressed out by all the demands of high school and the pressure to get into the perfect college. Whatever reasons led you to this book, I hope you will discover ideas and tips that will help you become more content with your life and confident in who you are.

Adolescence: A Self-Esteem Minefield

First, I want you to know that it's completely normal—and common—for teens to deal with self-esteem issues because you're in a unique and complicated position. You're trapped between two different worlds: leaving behind the world of childhood but not quite yet in the world of full-fledged adulthood. As a kid, you likely saw the world only through your own eyes. But as you got older, you started to consider how others view you. You started to worry about things like fitting in, being judged, and feeling accepted. Adolescence is a time when you start to make more of your own decisions and try to decide exactly who you are and how you fit into this world. This can be quite the challenge, especially when you consider all the other pressures and responsibilities that teenagers juggle—school, family, friends, relationships, sports, activities, jobs, parties, and how to respond to a world now filled with drugs, alcohol, and sexual activity. (Not to mention college applications and the pressure to figure out what you want to be when you grow up.) What teenager doesn't need a little help with everything on their plate?

As a teen, you're in a great place to learn these tools as you mature and explore your identity. By reading this book and engaging in these exercises, you're equipping yourself with the knowledge and insight that many don't discover until adulthood—or ever. When I teach self-esteem workshops to adults in my community, many people comment, "Why didn't we learn this stuff in school?" The fact is, most schools are so focused on academics and testing scores that they *don't* do their students justice when it comes to equipping them with the skills they need to really become confident, self-respecting individuals.

I think it's so cool that you're taking a step toward arming yourself with knowledge that will serve you well for the rest of your life. I'm so grateful that I have learned these tools over the years, and I often wish I could go back and see what it's like to spend a day in high school having the wisdom and self-esteem I have now. It is my sincere hope that, within the coming pages, you will learn some ways to better enjoy your time as a teen and journey through adulthood with confidence. These tools truly will help you cope with the stressors you face now and protect you from some of the struggles you might face down the road. So keep reading and get ready to feel happier and more confident!

A Peek Into What's to Come

Over the years, I've worked with many teens and have seen them build confidence and learn strategies to better handle the relationships and stressful circumstances in their lives. I will include some of their stories throughout the book to illustrate the ideas and exercises we will be exploring. (Note that names and identifying information have been changed to protect privacy.)

This book will include three parts: Part One will explore what self-esteem is and take a look at some of the many ways teens try to cope with overwhelming and confusing emotions. Part Two will give you tons of exercises that will help you build skills and explore concepts that play a role in the development of positive identity and healthy self-esteem. Part Three will include questions and concerns from a number of teens struggling with various issues related to self-esteem and challenges associated with adolescence.

Read this book and work through the exercises at your own pace. Improving self-esteem is an ongoing process that is something we all have to work on and keep in check throughout our lives. Be patient with yourself and know that you likely won't feel better or more confident immediately. Instead, it will be a gradual process as you give yourself time to work through each exercise and put new tools into practice. By reading this far, you've already begun investing in yourself, which is a huge step in building self-esteem. Give yourself credit and know that you're taking great steps toward creating a more rewarding future.

First Things First: The Facts About Self-Esteem

The phrase "self-esteem" has kind of gotten a bad rap over the years, and I bet a lot of teens groan at the thought of talking about it. And it's no wonder, because we often bring up self-esteem in reference to its negative form: low self-esteem. But the reality is that we all have self-esteem: It's just a matter of where our self-esteem falls on the spectrum of high to low. The word "esteem" means value, and self-esteem is about how much or how little you value yourself. In this section, we will explore what self-esteem is and why it's so important to have healthy self-esteem.

I view self-esteem on a continuum and tend to use the words "healthy self-esteem" to represent the higher end of the spectrum and "unhealthy self-esteem" to represent the lower end. Self-esteem doesn't stay the same: It can change throughout life and appear differently depending on the situation and who you're with. When you value yourself and believe in your worth, you have higher self-esteem and life becomes easier. But when you begin to judge yourself unfavorably, fall victim to the judgments of others, and obsess over whether you are acceptable and good enough, your self-esteem takes a nosedive and everything becomes more complicated. The goal for all of us is to establish a foundation of healthy self-esteem that is consistent and can be maintained across various situations and experiences throughout life.

What Is Healthy Self-Esteem?

There are many definitions of self-esteem. But the one we'll use is crafted just for teens and will be useful to keep in mind as you make your way through this book:

Healthy self-esteem is about consistently valuing who you are, feeling positive about your identity, having realistic expectations of yourself, and acting in ways that demonstrate self-respect and adherence to your own values.

In other words, building self-esteem is about learning to believe in your own worth and accept who you are: a human with both strengths and weaknesses, just like everyone else. By understanding that, you can begin to explore new ideas, learn new skills, and practice tools to move beyond insecurities and feel more confident.

Natalie's Story

Natalie's mom first brought her to see me when she was in middle school, saying they were really struggling at home. Natalie refused to ride the school bus in the morning, resulting in fights with her parents, who ultimately ended up having to drive her to school. Her mom said the issue was making her and her husband late for work and was causing a lot of friction in the family.

When I first met Natalie, she sat with her arms folded across her chest and responded to all my questions with one-word answers and shoulder shrugs. It was pretty clear she wasn't happy to be there. But after I explained that this was a safe space to discuss anything she wanted, Natalie softened a bit. She began telling me how awkward she felt at the bus stop where she waited with a group of popular girls who were in the grade above her. Natalie felt like a loser standing there alone while they laughed and gossiped about their peers, barely noticing her.

I empathized with what she was experiencing. Middle school and high school can be really rough socially! It's sometimes hard to find your place among the cliques and various groups of established friends.

Over the next few months Natalie and I worked on ways she could cope with the fear of being judged and armed her with skills to feel more comfortable at the bus stop. She didn't become close friends with that particular group of girls, but she got to the point where she could exchange friendly smiles with them each morning and in the hallways, which helped her feel less isolated and more comfortable being herself.

People with healthy self-esteem view themselves as worthwhile and good enough. They are able to recognize their positive qualities while also accepting that they are imperfect and will inevitably have flaws and face challenges and setbacks. They don't keep beating themselves up about their limitations. Instead, they just put things in perspective so that their imperfections don't drag them down.

People with healthy self-esteem are able to trust in their own judgment. They can express their own beliefs, wants, and needs without getting caught up with fear. They find healthy ways to deal with the chaos of peer pressure and avoid getting trapped in harmful patterns and destructive behaviors. They can recognize when relationships are unhealthy and dysfunctional, and they take steps to protect themselves by distancing themselves from toxic people.

People who are able to achieve a healthy level of self-esteem maintain realistic expectations of themselves and others. They feel deserving of respect, and they extend the same level of respect to others. They recognize that self-esteem comes from within, from a fundamental belief that you are okay, and that it can't be earned externally by seeking the approval or validation of others.

If, like most teens, your self-esteem is not in an optimal place, the idea of healthy self-esteem may seem like a lofty pipe dream. But I promise you, the awareness and new skills you will learn in this book—if you put them into practice—will land you on the path to becoming the happy, confident, self-assured person you want to be.

What You Stand to Gain from Healthy Self-Esteem

Improving your self-esteem has many benefits, like being able to trust in yourself and follow your own instincts. You can take pride in your accomplishments and feel a sense of purpose and hope for the future. You learn to feel comfortable in your own skin and make decisions without always relying on everyone else to decide for you. You become more self-assured and less likely to procrastinate or second-guess your opinions and choices. For example, if your friends ask you what movie you want to see, you are able to give your honest opinion without fear that it won't be what they want to see. When self-esteem is healthy, you worry less about what everyone else thinks and rise above feelings of self-doubt and fear.

As self-esteem improves, you can avoid getting caught up in a cycle of self-blame and negative thinking. You can accept your mistakes, knowing that they are inevitable in life and provide valuable lessons and opportunities for growth. You are able to recognize that the effort you put in is just as important, if not more so, than the end result. If you get a C on a test, for example, instead of beating yourself up for not getting an A, you recognize that either you did the best you could or maybe didn't study hard enough. You can then decide to get extra help or study more in the future. When your self-esteem is intact, you are able to view one bad grade or failed class as a disappointment but not the end of the world.

It also means you're able to find a stable balance of independence and interdependence. You can enjoy spending time alone but also form relationships that are healthy and secure rather than clingy or overbearing. You come to expect honesty and equality in relationships as you establish healthy boundaries, which sets you up to have better experiences when it comes to dating and friendships. People with high self-esteem are less likely to be manipulated or treated poorly by others, and they know when to walk away from an unhealthy situation. They also communicate well with others and are assertive in situations where they need to speak up, including asking for help without feelings of shame or embarrassment.

Positive self-esteem enables you to interact in healthy ways with others and avoid engaging in behaviors like bullying, teasing, or putting others down in a misguided attempt to feel powerful or liked. Instead, you know and follow your own values, and you can make your own choices without succumbing to peer pressure or becoming paralyzed by fear of being judged. You are able to navigate the new experiences and temptations that high school brings with confidence rather than anxiety about fitting in. Friendships are fulfilling and fun rather than overwhelming and filled with drama and chaos. You're able to say "no" and stand your ground without feeling like a loser or fearing rejection.

Another great thing about positive self-esteem is that you can better balance everything you have on your plate because you will develop the skills to better manage the stress and pressures that are so prevalent in high school. Basically, improving self-esteem can help you like yourself more and go through life more comfortably and with a greater sense of security in who you are.

What Self-Esteem Is Not

Healthy self-esteem isn't about conforming to what other people want you to be.

It's not about trying to be just like everyone else. In adolescence, there's a huge amount of pressure to fit in and find your place among various groups of kids. We all want to be seen and accepted by others, but self-esteem doesn't come from external approval.

It's also not about being flawless and well liked. Or being "perfect" or the most popular person at school. It's about accepting who you are and seeing yourself as equal in worth to everyone else. Healthy self-esteem doesn't mean that we don't have weaknesses—it involves recognizing that we all have problem areas, insecurities, and moments of vulnerability, even if they are not obvious to the outside world. For example, the girl in your class who seems super confident and able to talk to the most popular guys in school with ease probably struggles with her own insecurities, even if it's not so obvious what they might be. And the kid who has a bunch of friends but makes fun of all the less popular students? Deep down, he probably *doesn't* really feel all that great about himself.

You see, there are lots of ways to mask or ineffectively deal with low self-esteem. Many people put up a front, pretending like things are great. They smile and laugh at school but go home to isolate themselves in their room, sleeping a lot and bottling up their emotions. Sometimes people become arrogant or turn into bullies, putting others down in unproductive attempts to build themselves up.

Some teens become imprisoned by self-esteem issues, isolating themselves or turning to self-harmful behaviors as a way to cope. Some turn to the wrong crowd or spiral into destructive behaviors in hope that acting in certain ways will make them appear cool or get them the recognition and approval they crave. They falsely believe that being liked by others will help them feel better about who they are.

But healthy self-esteem is not the same as hiding insecurities, adopting a new identity, or distracting from your own imperfections by drawing attention to the weaknesses of others. It's not about bragging about your own accomplishments or possessions to gain approval or popularity, nor is it about trying to make others like you. It's about learning to like yourself.

Scott's Story

Scott came to see me after his parents decided they'd had enough of his changing behavior and wanted to figure out what was going on. He was a bright and likable kid, but his life had taken a turn for the worse in recent months. Normally a great student, Scott was doing poorly that quarter. He started hanging out with a different group of kids and was introduced to alcohol, vaping, and marijuana.

One weekend when his parents were out of town, Scott threw a huge party, inviting everyone he knew to his house. According to him, it was a huge success. Tons of kids showed up, and many brought drugs. That night, Scott flirted with several girls, and a few guys thanked him for throwing such an awesome, unchaperoned party. Although Scott spent all of Sunday cleaning up the house, making sure it was back in perfect order before his parents returned, his parents still found out about the party when a neighbor mentioned they'd seen a large group of teens outside the house at 2 a.m., including an intoxicated girl who was throwing up in the bushes. Scott confessed about the party to his parents, though he could not give them an acceptable explanation as to what compelled him to go behind their backs.

In our sessions, Scott talked about how badly he wanted to be seen as cool. For most of his life, people had seen Scott as "the good kid." He got great grades, was adored by teachers, and was well liked by the parents of all his peers. But when Scott got rejected after asking the girl he liked to the homecoming dance and then heard her giggling about him with her group of friends, he started to wonder if there was really any benefit to being the good guy. It seemed like all the girls in his school were going after the "bad boys"— the ones who threw crazy parties or sold drugs. Scott wondered if he'd have better luck in dating if he tried to become more like those guys. That's when he had decided to throw the party.

The problem was, nothing really changed after the party. A few more people smiled and acknowledged him in the hallways, but Scott still felt down about his prospects in dating and his future on the whole. He began to wonder if the party was worth the tension he'd created at home. We started looking at the reasons he decided to throw the party and about his need to feel liked by others. I helped Scott explore the beliefs he held about himself, and I taught him about the importance of building self-esteem. He started to see that in order for the girls he liked to be attracted to him, he first had to feel worthy of their attention *himself*.

You won't find healthy self-esteem externally in the attention or approval of others. It's something that must come from within—from changing your internal feelings about who you are and knowing you truly are good enough, despite what life or other people throw your way. No matter how many "fans" you have, their opinion of you won't improve your self-esteem. You have to improve it from the inside out.

Self-Esteem Is Not the Same as Arrogance

People seeking self-improvement sometimes worry that building self-esteem will make them arrogant or self-absorbed. Arrogant and narcissistic people *appear* to be confident in who they are, and they seem to think they are better than everyone else. But this egotistical nature is a mask for low self-esteem. Arrogant people *act* in selfish or superior ways in an ineffective attempt to improve their feelings of self-worth. This rarely works. Putting others down may provide temporary feelings of self-importance because they get attention or laughs, but deep down, bullies and arrogant people feel unworthy and inadequate. And trying to fill that void at the expense of others never works: It just strengthens their feelings of being fundamentally flawed.

People with healthy self-esteem are able to be nice to everyone, including themselves. High self-esteem allows you to acknowledge that *everyone* has inherent worth and feel good about yourself while also demonstrating mutual respect and positive regard for others. This is very different from arrogance.

The Confidence Curve

A lot of people confuse the concepts of self-esteem and self-confidence. Although similar, they aren't the same thing. Self-esteem is about how you feel about your total core self as a *whole*. Confidence is how capable and self-assured you feel about yourself in a specific area. Confidence will inevitably vary based on your individual skills and talents, and it's normal to feel confidence in some areas but not others. But when you lack belief or trust in yourself regarding a particular skill or task, do you allow that lack of confidence to influence your feelings of self-worth?

For example, imagine you go bowling with a group of friends. You have only bowled once or twice in your life, so your confidence in your ability to bowl strikes each turn will likely be fairly low. But how do you feel about yourself overall? Do you feel embarrassed that you aren't better and beat yourself up about your subpar bowling skills? Or do you avoid judgment from yourself and others and recognize that you're all just there to have fun?

As another example, imagine two people at a dance. Both lack confidence in their dancing skills, but one has healthy self-esteem and the other does not. The person with high self-esteem is able to have fun with their friends, busting out moves and acting silly on the dance floor, unfazed by what other people think. But the person with low self-esteem may not even set foot on the dance floor, fearing that everyone will notice how ridiculous they look. Low self-esteem holds us back and makes us dwell on our insecurities or low levels of confidence. Healthy self-esteem allows us to see beyond moments of self-doubt and enjoy life without unnecessary fear.

When self-esteem is low, a lack of confidence can reinforce feelings of insecurity. But when it's high, we can view our lack of confidence in certain areas as a normal part of life. We can choose to put our energy into improving in that area instead of dwelling on things we aren't good at. People with healthy self-esteem recognize that weaknesses are inevitable and a lack of confidence in certain areas does not translate to feeling unworthy or not good enough.

CHECK IN WITH YOURSELF

Now that we've discussed some differences between healthy and unhealthy self-esteem, take a moment to check in with yourself to see where your level of self-esteem may fall. Below are several statements that encompass characteristics and beliefs of teens with healthy self-esteem, followed by a list of problems and patterns that are common for people with low self-esteem. Check off any items that you identify with on each list:

Healthy Self-Esteem

☐ I am worthy.

☐ I am capable.

☐ I can handle challenges and setbacks.

☐ I take pride in my strengths and accomplishments.

☐ I can accept my weaknesses.

☐ I am okay with imperfection.

☐ I accept and learn from mistakes.

☐ I don't need to prove myself to anyone.

☐ I am proud of my efforts.

☐ I take responsibility for my own actions.

☐ I am able to make decisions.

☐ I can make choices without the influence of peer pressure.

☐ I am able to stand up for and protect myself.

☐ I can avoid getting wrapped up in gossip.

☐ I sometimes enjoy being alone.

☐ I am comfortable in group settings.

☐ I am able to think for myself.

☐ I am able to ask for help when necessary.

☐ I am able to accept compliments.

☐ I am able to handle criticism.

☐ I don't fixate on the judgments of others.

☐ My relationships are generally healthy and fulfilling.

☐ I am able to set limits and boundaries.

☐ I am able to effectively communicate with others.

☐ I have realistic expectations and standards.

☐ I am happy with my values and principles.

- [ ] I am able to handle stress.
- [ ] I am able to self-soothe.
- [ ] I am able to handle disappointment or grief.
- [ ] My life has meaning or purpose.

Unhealthy Self-Esteem

- [ ] I spend a lot of time worried about what others think.
- [ ] I frequently doubt myself.
- [ ] I often feel a sense of shame.
- [ ] I have difficulty making decisions.
- [ ] I often procrastinate.
- [ ] I tend to blame others when things don't go my way or work out.
- [ ] I often feel like a victim.
- [ ] I often feel anxious or depressed.
- [ ] I often feel guilty.
- [ ] I need to be perfect.
- [ ] I often find myself apologizing.
- [ ] I often feel like a burden.
- [ ] I have difficulty relying on others or asking for help.
- [ ] I have difficulty making eye contact with others.
- [ ] I believe other people's thoughts and opinions are more important than mine.
- [ ] I often feel taken advantage of by others.
- [ ] I often feel left out of groups.
- [ ] I find it difficult to end toxic or abusive relationships.
- [ ] I easily succumb to peer pressure.
- [ ] I engage in behaviors that I know are unhealthy.
- [ ] I rely on others to make me feel good.
- [ ] I frequently seek approval from others.
- [ ] I crave reassurance and compliments.
- [ ] I find it very difficult when others are mad or upset with me.
- [ ] I have difficulty hearing criticism, whether constructive or otherwise.
- [ ] I feel uncomfortable when people compliment me.
- [ ] I frequently compare myself to others.
- [ ] I find it hard to speak up for myself.
- [ ] I have trouble managing stress.
- [ ] I often become overwhelmed.

Give yourself credit for any checks you made on the healthy self-esteem list and use the checks on the unhealthy self-esteem list to identify areas you will want to pay particular attention to as you work on improving your self-esteem. In Part Two, we will revisit these checklists as you begin learning strategies to become more self-assured.

Protect Your Rights!

As a human, we all have basic rights, but we aren't always aware of what these rights are. Or sometimes when self-esteem is low, we don't believe these rights could possibly apply to us. Maybe it was the environment or culture you grew up in or certain experiences you've faced that prevented you from developing a belief in these rights or caused you to separate yourself from some of these inherent principles. Part of working to build self-esteem will involve claiming these rights and developing an understanding that these principles do apply to you just as much as they do anyone else.

Sometimes it's especially tricky to believe in your rights when you are a minor. Let's face it: You really *can't* make all your own decisions. Legally, your parents or guardians have a major say in what you can or can't do. Teachers, principals, and other authority figures play a role in enforcing various rules and making decisions that you are expected to follow. You may not have total control over all your options and choices, but you still have several rights that apply to how you think, feel, and act.

If your cultural background differs from that of mainstream American culture, you might face some additional challenges in terms of believing in and asserting these rights. You might also need to spend some extra time adapting them to fit within your own family system. Whether or not others believe in or respect your rights, the important thing is that you believe in them for yourself. When others disrespect you or violate your rights, you understand that it is about their ignorance, their own history, or their rigid ways of thinking, not your value or worth.

The following is a list of your basic rights. As you read over it, note any items that feel particularly foreign or difficult for you to believe. These items will indicate areas where you may need to focus the most attention along your journey to improving your self-esteem.

MY PERSONAL RIGHTS AS A TEEN

1. I have the right to be happy and believe in my unlimited and unconditional worth, no matter how anyone else treats me or makes me feel.

2. I have the right to make mistakes and accept my imperfections, knowing we all have flaws and weaknesses and that mistakes are part of growing and learning.

3. I have the right to create my own value system and establish beliefs that may differ from those of others.

4. I have the right to respectfully express my own opinions, beliefs, and needs, even if they are in disagreement with or rejected by others.

5. I have the right to disagree with rules and authority figures and respectfully express my own thoughts, knowing that doing so may not always result in the outcome I hope for.

6. I have the right to protect myself, say "no," and resist temptations and peer pressure that will not serve me well.

7. I have the right to respect my body, expect respect from others, say "no" to unwanted advances, and make decisions regarding my sexuality.

8. I have the right to be unique and express myself as I choose so long as I don't offend or violate the rights of others.

9. I have the right to establish boundaries with others, set limits, and stand for myself as I appreciate my individual identity.

10. I have the right to change my mind, grow, and allow myself to figure out who I want to be as I mature into adulthood.

Coping: What Not to Do

Low self-esteem often goes hand in hand with depression and anxiety, and it can be especially difficult for teens to figure out how to cope. When you were younger, your parents likely noticed if something was off and they may have addressed it by talking to your teacher, school counselor, or doctor to figure out the problem and get help. Now, chances are, you're more independent and less reliant on your parents to monitor you as you mature, but you aren't quite independent enough to get outside help on your own.

Maybe you haven't felt comfortable talking about your struggles with your family, or perhaps you've tried and been met with responses like, "It's normal to feel this way as a teen," "You'll get over it," or "Just snap out of it." But the truth is, many teens face emotions that aren't necessarily a normal part of adolescence and are indicative of underlying problems related to a mood disorder or very poor self-esteem. Without intervention or outside help, they're left to cope with feelings of stress, sadness, or identity confusion on their own. And lack of support and suitable guidance puts you at risk of turning to coping mechanisms that are unhealthy and ultimately ineffective.

Sasha's Story

Sasha felt isolated and alone at school and asked her parents if she could talk to a therapist. When she came to see me, she told me she hated her high school. She felt like an outsider, barely talking to anyone in her classes and never being invited to parties. She wanted to make friends but found it impossible to forge her way into the already-established friend groups at her school. She felt like a loser, never knowing what to say to people—except when she was online.

In the world of the Internet, Sasha found a place where she fit in. It was much easier to chat with people she met online via a profile name and her best possible profile picture versus in person at school where she felt awkward and uncertain. If she felt at all uncomfortable or ran out of funny things to say, she could easily type "G2G" or simply stop responding.

In our sessions, she excitedly told me stories about some of the friends she was meeting online. I had to admit, Sasha's depression seemed to be lifting as she found support and connections with others she could open up to.

Soon, however, I received an email from Sasha's mom stating she was very concerned. While putting away laundry, Sasha's mom had found razor blades in her drawer and subsequently learned that Sasha was cutting herself. When Sasha and I discussed her mother's email in our next session, she revealed self-harm was something she had tried a few times. She told me how Reema, one of her Tumblr friends, had reblogged a poem about cutting. The poem spoke to Sasha because she finally felt like somebody else understood her pain.

Learning that others were using cutting to relieve their overwhelming feelings of depression, Sasha decided to give it a try. "It's not the same as suicide," she told me. "My mom doesn't get that. And it's not about getting attention either. I know some people do it for attention, but I didn't want anyone to know. I just wanted to see if it would make me feel better."

I empathized with Sasha, but I also educated her that cutting becomes a highly addictive habit with many undesirable consequences. Over time, cutting doesn't produce the high it initially did, and people need to cut more and deeper to achieve the same relief they've become desperate for. This becomes dangerous and only adds to their problems.

Luckily for Sasha, her cutting was discovered early on before it snowballed into a major addictive behavior. We were able to work together on tackling the root issues behind her desire to cut and to equip her with healthier coping tools that were more effective than those she heard about from friends who were also struggling.

Self-Harm

When people engage in risky or self-harmful behaviors, it's often due to a need to gain a sense of control. For example, somebody who feels emotionally powerless in some aspect of their life might try to obtain control the only way they feel able—by controlling what they do physically. Cutting is now one of the most prevalent methods of self-injury among teens, and it can be an especially perplexing issue for parents who discover it. Many people cannot comprehend why anyone would want to cause themselves pain, and uninformed adults often worry that cutting equals a wish to die.

But cutting isn't the same as a suicide attempt—it's a way that people try to gain relief from intense emotional pain by creating physical pain instead. As Sasha discovered, however, cutting only creates a temporary distraction from dealing with the real issues. Rather than solve the root problem, it creates more problems, resulting in lasting scars, shame, secrecy, and potential complications that may require medical attention.

Some teens inflict self-harm in less extreme ways, such as hitting themselves, punching walls, pulling their hair out, etc. But if these self-harming behaviors do provide relief, the effects are only temporary. Over time, the relief begins to wear off, leaving the person with the urge to self-harm *even more*. Self-harm is addictive and destructive, and it often creates a trap of patterns that are very difficult to break. It also reinforces low self-esteem by sending subtle messages to yourself that you do not value your body or your well-being. If you are using self-harm as a way to cope, your first priority should be to get help in identifying the triggers that lead to self-injury and begin establishing healthier ways of coping.

Seeking Guidance from Peers and Social Media

Some teens attempt to cope with their issues by connecting with others who seem to share common struggles. Social media and the Internet can be great places to find people who have the same interests or relate to the same problems. But they can also be places of misguided information and uninformed individuals giving bad advice. So many of the teens I have worked with have found solace in meeting new friends and developing friendships virtually, but sometimes they can be more harmful than helpful.

On the one hand, all humans are eager for connection, and social support can be a wonderful thing during times of stress or sadness. Technology opens doors to tons of people we may not otherwise meet, and it feels safe because of the anonymity it can provide. On the other hand, it has its dangers, and it's important to be cautious when taking advice from people who are ultimately strangers and potentially just as stuck as you are. It's easy for a teen who is feeling isolated and utterly alone at school to turn to online groups or others who seem to relate, especially if they're the only places they feel like they can fit in or seek advice on how to feel better.

Online friendships and groups can feel very enticing when they offer hope and unconditional acceptance, but it's important to be cautious and informed when exploring these groups, making new friendships, and following advice regarding ways to cope. Ask yourself—is this really in my best interest in the long run? Does this new friendship feel like a true and healthy bond, or am I grasping at straws to make a connection and find validation? Are the people I'm talking to qualified to give sound advice? Or are they just as lost as I'm feeling?

The same advice goes for evaluating the people you spend time with in person. Middle school and high school can bring about many changes in people—for better or worse—and these changes can sometimes impact friendships. You may find yourself growing apart from the people you were best friends with as a child, or you may gravitate toward different types of friendships—and that's okay. You are allowed to grow and forge new paths, but stop to consider the reasons for doing so. Are you drawn to a new crowd because of new interests or because of an aspiration to find answers to the problems you are dealing with? Are you following an old friend or holding onto relationships that have become toxic because you feel unable to make your own choices and find your own way? Or are you choosing friendships that help you be your best self? Healthy self-esteem will help you make smart decisions when it comes to friendships and protect you from stumbling down a path that creates more problems.

Sex, Drugs, and Alcohol

Teens who are struggling with depression, anxiety, or low self-esteem sometimes get overly involved in potentially risky things, or they seek pleasure that will distract them from their pain. Typical teenage experiences like sex, drugs, and alcohol can spiral out of control when they are used as a means to escape. Peer pressure can be difficult to navigate when you lack the confidence and self-assurance to say "no." Turning to drugs or alcohol—or acting in promiscuous ways to gain approval and acceptance—can lead to devastating consequences that only derail your chances of feeling happy and disrupt your progress in building self-esteem.

I've worked with many teens who have experimented with drugs after hearing friends are using them—whether legally or illegally—to manage their anxiety or obtain better focus in school. Often these people are smart individuals who promise they have done the research and have come to believe these drugs are in their best interest. The Internet will turn up all sorts of research on why one particular drug or another may actually be advisable and less damaging than the anti-drug campaigns might have you believe. But self-medicating without the guidance of a medical professional is never a good idea. It's always better to have your symptoms evaluated by somebody who can point you in the best possible direction toward feeling better.

I know it's unrealistic to advise you to avoid things like drinking and exploring sexually. After all, adolescence is a time for exploring new things, developing new relationships, and dipping your toe into new experiences as you mature. But I urge you to think about your reasons for getting involved in activities and behaviors that could be risky. Try to make smart choices from a place of strength rather than an impulse driven by peer pressure or a desire to be accepted. When you make your own decisions for the right reasons, you reinforce healthy self-esteem, but ignoring your inner wisdom and acting impulsively destroys it.

Disordered Eating

Disordered eating is another pattern rooted in control that can lead to serious consequences that require medical attention. Teens who feel powerless when facing their overwhelming, negative emotions might focus on eating and exercise as a way to regain some sense of control. Although dieting or exercise may start out innocently enough, you can start to feel obsessive about the sense of control. Things can rapidly spiral downward into serious eating disorders that are life-threating and require intensive treatment programs to overcome. If you have been engaging in disordered eating or are struggling with body image issues, find a qualified professional to help you get back on a healthy track. See the resources section (pages 134 to 136) to find help.

Avoiding or Masking

For some, avoiding, dwelling on, or drawing attention to the problem may be the only way they know how to deal with confusing or negative feelings. Faking happiness and self-confidence may work temporarily, whether it's through extreme measures like bullying others or just putting on a happy front (as discussed on pages 4, 5, and 7). But in the long run, avoidance of the issues only makes them grow worse. In reality, when there is a difference between what people show the outside world and what they really feel on the inside, it can cause them to become depressed. Part of building self-esteem involves being honest with yourself about your true feelings and developing the courage to make changes.

Assessing Your Current Ways of Coping

There are many ways to cope with life's stressors, and an important first step in improving self-esteem is learning what your current coping methods are and considering whether they are healthy. The exercises in Part Two will guide you in developing your own arsenal of healthy coping skills. Think about the methods you currently use to deal with stress. Could any be considered harmful? Are they meant to solve problems or distract you from them? Will they ultimately move you in the direction of healing and feeling better? Or do they have the potential to create additional problems?

Write about any potentially unhealthy coping methods that may be creating more harm than good:

_____

_____

_____

_____

_____

As you look back on your responses, are there any things you hope to change? How could you cut back on using unhealthy coping strategies? I am not suggesting you quit these unhealthy methods cold turkey, because trying to do so might create more stress. But by simply identifying what they are, you can gain more awareness around changes you might want to make as you move forward with your self-esteem goals.

WHEN TO GET HELP

There are many ineffective, dangerous, and potentially life-threatening ways that people deal with stress, low self-esteem, and feelings of depression or anxiety. If you are engaging in any particularly self-destructive behaviors, identify with any of the symptoms or experiences in the following checklist, or find yourself feeling overwhelmed and unable to work through the exercises in this book on your own, please reach out to a qualified professional to help guide you through the process and support you in healing.

Issues that will likely require the help of a professional:

☐ Thoughts about suicide

☐ Self-harm

☐ Self-medicating

☐ Major depression

☐ Severe anxiety

☐ Extreme mood swings

☐ Unresolved grief

☐ Physical abuse

☐ Emotional abuse

☐ Sexual abuse

☐ Incest

☐ Severely restricted eating

☐ Binging or purging

☐ Exercise obsession

☐ Drug or alcohol addiction

☐ Promiscuous behaviors

☐ Truancy

If you are unable to talk to a parent or guardian about getting help because they're unwilling to listen, unsupportive of therapy, or somehow inflicting abuse or harm on you, consider confiding in your school counselor or another adult you can trust. Get help. You are worth it!

Facing Fear, Doubt, and the Uncertainties of Change

Battling low self-esteem can be challenging, regardless of how bad or severe your experiences are. You may not identify with any items on the previous checklist, and you may not have any unhealthy coping techniques. If that's the case, you might be wondering how you could possibly still feel so terribly lost. It doesn't matter why you landed in the place where you are. The fact is, you are still suffering, and that's totally normal. We don't need to completely understand how we developed low self-esteem in order to change it. People often get stuck trying to find the cause, or they become trapped in feelings of guilt and unworthiness, fearing that they aren't *bad enough* to deserve or require help. You don't have to experience a terrible childhood or pinpoint a traumatic event to have low self-esteem. You deserve the chance to feel good about who you are and have a happy future, so put aside any doubts that make you question whether self-esteem help is right for you.

Envision suffering to be like gas filling a container—no matter how big or small the container is, the gas will spread and eventually fill the whole space. I like to use this analogy to demonstrate that there really is no point in comparing our own suffering or problems to those of others. Instead of questioning whether your own struggles are bad enough to require attention, put your energy into actively doing what you can to make a change and feel better.

People with low self-esteem may not always share the same reasons behind their insecurities and feelings of unworthiness, but they share a common thread—they live with the fear that they are not good enough and that they are somehow fundamentally flawed. This fear can hold you back from achieving your goals. But it can be overcome, and you can find ways to improve how you feel about yourself in order to achieve a more fulfilling life.

It's completely normal to experience some skepticism about whether this book can help you. Change, even if it's for the better, can be scary. Part of building self-esteem involves creating new habits and breaking free from some of the previous patterns that have held you back. This new way of being may bring some feelings of resistance or apprehension, and that is to be expected.

Annie came to see me due to failing grades, conflict with her parents, and fights with her friends. As I learned about her life, it was clear to me that she'd grown up—and was living amid—chaos and dysfunction due to both of her parents' heavy drinking. Low self-esteem and a lack of effective communication skills were at the root of many of Annie's uncertainties regarding how to handle herself—and it led her to make many poor choices.

As Annie started focusing on what she wanted and who she wanted to be, she began to recognize how years of dysfunction in her family contributed to her struggles and difficulty maintaining a healthy sense of self. Annie started working to disengage from the conflict at home and learned to walk away from arguments when her parents had been drinking. She realized that conflict felt normal to her, and that's why she frequently created drama with friends. Recognizing that this wasn't ultimately effective, Annie became eager to learn new ways of being.

She worked hard to put tools to improve her self-esteem into practice and began to communicate in more effective ways. Soon, she started experiencing more happiness and a greater sense of calm. But these new feelings started to feel uncomfortable. They felt strange and somewhat scary, because she felt like she was always waiting for the other shoe to drop.

Dysfunction had been the only thing she'd known so it was challenging to feel content with things being okay. Annie needed to accept that change was sometimes hard and that it would take some time to get used to a new normal that involved stability and lack of chaos.

As you approach each exercise in the coming pages, know that it's normal to experience some feelings of uneasiness as you explore new ideas and begin embracing your own self-worth. Sometimes when you dive deeper into understanding your struggles, things feel worse before they get better. Know that this is okay, and don't let it discourage you. Remember you have to walk through the storm to get to the rainbow.

Sometimes, even positive changes feel awkward and foreign. We become comfortable with what is familiar, and stepping outside our comfort zone is challenging. So when you do experience feelings of discomfort, fear, or doubt, remember that it's just part of the process. Rather than feeling frustrated and trying to dismiss these feelings, just notice they're there. Accept them and remind yourself that it's necessary to work through them to move forward.

Try It Now

Write about any initial fears you have regarding working through this book or improving self-esteem:

_____

_____

_____

_____

_____

_____

_____

_____

_____

_____

_____

_____

_____

You Are Enough

Overcoming fear involves having the courage to believe you are worth it. It may be especially challenging to decide to make changes because years of low self-esteem have led you to believe you don't have any value but this simply is not true. That's just the depression and lack of self-esteem talking. The reality is, we all have intrinsic worth, but this can be a tricky concept for people to wrap their brains around. It may even contradict things you've felt about yourself for years. The hard thing about building self-esteem is that doing so involves becoming nicer to yourself and implementing more healthy ways of taking care of yourself. When you don't feel worthy, it can be hard to take these first steps. So I'm going to ask you to put aside your doubts and quiet that voice inside your head telling you, "She can't be talking to *me!* No way I have *worth!*" and just trust me as we go on this journey together.

You have worth, you are enough, and you deserve to believe it. I know that more work can seem daunting when you already have a bunch of schoolwork and other responsibilities on your plate. But bear with me! I promise that improving your self-esteem will be worthwhile and serve you well for the rest of your life. It will set you up to experience more joy and to have more rewarding experiences both now and well into your adult years.

You Can Feel Better

Remember that your current level of self-esteem isn't written in stone: It is something you can change and improve. Not only will building self-esteem help you feel more confident and content with your identity, it will help you deal with many of the negative emotional symptoms that you may be experiencing. One thing I love about self-esteem building tools is that they are the same tools used to help fight depression and anxiety. There are so many benefits to putting effort into building self-esteem. With this book, you will feel better as you boost your confidence and create a more stable and sustainable level of self-esteem.

Take your time as you work through the exercises. Remember that building self-esteem begins on the inside by developing an awareness of the various ways you think about yourself and discovering who you really are. Recognize that you can't develop confidence or find self-acceptance by gaining the approval of others or worrying about things like your appearance, performance, or ability to fit in. Developing self-esteem will require you to go below the surface and take a deeper look inside. It will involve exploring your belief systems and developing a willingness to change some of the opinions you've held in the past. Try to stay open to learning new skills and work hard to put them into practice. With some time and effort, you will feel better. So let's begin!

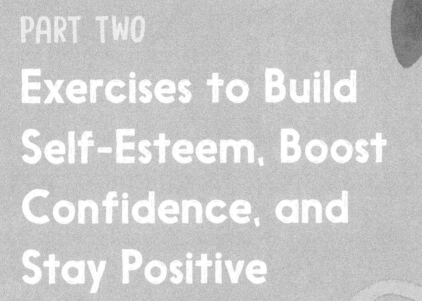

PART TWO

Exercises to Build Self-Esteem, Boost Confidence, and Stay Positive

This section includes exercises that will help you assess your level of self-esteem and explore concepts related to developing a more positive outlook and greater confidence in your identity. You will learn ideas for healthy coping mechanisms and acquire new skills that will be useful along your journey to creating a healthier, more rewarding sense of self.

Remember that building self-esteem is a process that takes time. Some of these exercises may seem easy on paper but will likely be harder to put into practice in the real world. Be patient with yourself. You may want to work through one exercise at a time, giving yourself a few days or weeks before answering any questions related to your observations. Or you may want to plow through several and revisit follow-up questions later once you've had plenty of opportunities to put these new skills to use. Everybody's experience with these exercises will be different, so pace yourself as you see fit. The more time you invest, the greater the benefits you will see.

BASELINE SELF-ESTEEM SURVEY

As previously mentioned, self-esteem is something that can change throughout your life, as various experiences impact how you feel about your own personal worth.

On the continuum below, plot where you feel your self-esteem currently falls:

LOW SELF-ESTEEM ⟵————————————————⟶ HIGH SELF-ESTEEM

Why do you think your self-esteem falls where it does?

_____

_____

_____

_____

_____

How does it feel to see where you plotted your level of self-esteem?

_____

_____

_____

_____

_____

A Peek Back at the Self-Esteem Checklists

Look back over the items you checked on the healthy versus unhealthy self-esteem checklists on pages 9 and 10. Consider whether you were surprised by anything you selected in either category and see if you can pinpoint which items contribute most to your current level of self-esteem. Which items do you most need to improve? Write about your observations here:

_____

_____

_____

_____

_____

My Self-Esteem Goals

The main goal of this book is to build and maintain healthy self-esteem across all areas of your life, but each individual's journey will be specific to their own needs. Think about the personal goals you have in regard to raising your self-esteem. What would you like to be different? What do you hope to achieve after working through this book?

_____

_____

_____

_____

_____

FINDING FAITH IN YOURSELF

Building self-esteem will require some faith in yourself. Even if you plotted your self-esteem at the very low end of the continuum, the good news is that by reading this book, you clearly have at least a small seed of hope that building your self-esteem is possible and worthwhile. So allow that part to push you forward as we examine your self-doubt.

Faith in Yourself Quiz

Answer "true" or "false" to the following questions:

I trust myself to ...

1.	Make good decisions.	True	False
2.	Share my opinions and ideas.	True	False
3.	Speak up for myself.	True	False
4.	Take healthy risks.	True	False
5.	Say "no" to things that can harm me.	True	False
6.	Care for my own well-being.	True	False
7.	Engage in healthy relationships.	True	False
8.	Walk away from harmful relationships.	True	False
9.	Take credit for my accomplishments.	True	False
10.	Ask for help when needed.	True	False
11.	Avoid procrastination.	True	False
12.	Set realistic goals.	True	False
13.	Put new tools I learn into practice.	True	False
14.	Stay motivated to build self-esteem.	True	False

If you answered "true" to most of the above questions, congratulations! Building self-esteem may be a little easier for you than it is for most people. But if you answered mostly "false," that's completely normal. Most people with low self-esteem find it hard to make decisions, take good care of themselves, establish healthy relationships, and find the motivation to take the necessary steps to make positive changes. This book is designed to help you learn how to do exactly these things.

Recruiting a Friend

If in the previous assessment you answered "false" to trusting yourself when it comes to putting new tools into practice or staying motivated to build self-esteem, consider enlisting the help of a friend who might benefit from working through this book with you. Sometimes simply stating your goals out loud can be motivating.

Identify three people you could potentially share your self-esteem building goals with:

_____

_____

_____

What reservations do you have about opening up to others regarding your self-esteem goals?

_____

_____

_____

Try sharing your goals with one person and reflect on how it goes:

_____

_____

_____

TRACKING A TIMELINE OF EVENTS

We may not always be able to identify where low self-esteem stems from, but sometimes we can recognize various events and experiences that likely impacted our sense of self. Think about any significant or major events you recall from your past, plot them on the timeline below, and consider the following questions for each time period.

During this time period:	INFANCY	TODDLER	PRESCHOOL
What were the significant events you experienced?			
How were you perceived?			
What was your overall emotional experience?			
Do you recall feeling confident or filled with self-doubt?			
What events or experiences had the greatest impact on your self-esteem?			

The Ultimate Self-Esteem Workbook for Teens

ELEMENTARY   MIDDLE SCHOOL   HIGH SCHOOL

NOTICING NEGATIVE SELF-TALK

One of the best tools to build self-esteem, fight depression, and decrease anxiety involves learning to pay attention to your own self-talk. Self-talk refers to the constant stream of thoughts, both conscious and subconscious, going through your mind all day long. The problem for most of us is that our self-talk tends to be overwhelmingly negative and filled with self-critical or anxiety-provoking messages. In order to feel better, we need to learn to control our self-talk and ensure that it includes messages that are optimistic and encouraging.

Distorted and Irrational Thinking

Negative self-talk includes distorted messages and irrational thoughts that typically fall into the following distinct categories. Read over each description and think about when you engage in these problematic ways of thinking:

BLACK-AND-WHITE THINKING	MINIMIZATION
Black-and-white or all-or-nothing thinking is when you think in extreme ways. Things are either all good or all bad.	Minimization is when you downplay the importance of your strengths and accomplishments.
EXAMPLES:	EXAMPLES:
That test was hard. I am going to fail the class. She ignored my text. Everyone hates me. Nothing ever works out for me.	I've done well so far, but I might mess up and fail the class. I got a 90% on the test. I can't believe I didn't get a perfect score. They invited me to the party because they feel sorry for me.
I DO THIS WHEN:	I DO THIS WHEN:
_____ _____ _____	_____ _____ _____

CATASTROPHIZING

Catastrophizing is when you magnify the negatives. You dwell on mistakes and blow problems out of proportion.

EXAMPLES:

Since I made this mistake, I should probably just quit.

He broke up with me. I'm probably never going to find happiness.

I failed this exam and will never get into any colleges.

I DO THIS WHEN:

_____

_____

_____

PERSONALIZATION

Personalization is when you always assume responsibility for anything that goes wrong.

EXAMPLES:

It's my fault my friends aren't talking to me.

I always ruin everything.

I'm just not smart enough.

I DO THIS WHEN:

_____

_____

_____

MIND READING AND JUMPING TO CONCLUSIONS

Mind reading and jumping to conclusions are assumptions that others are negatively judging you without valid reasons or you fixate on the worst-case scenario as your default.

EXAMPLES:

I'm going to fail and things are never going to work out.

They don't really like me. They just feel sorry for me.

I can't be happy if she doesn't want to be with me.

I DO THIS WHEN:

_____

_____

_____

LABELING

Labeling is when you assign yourself negative labels or call yourself mean names.

EXAMPLES:

I'm such an idiot.

I'm an incompetent failure.

I'm a freak.

I DO THIS WHEN:

_____

_____

_____

Thinking in these negative ways creates a pessimistic attitude that makes it hard to feel good and to maintain healthy self-esteem. Sometimes you even set yourself up for failure as the statements become self-fulfilling prophecies. By monitoring your thinking and working to change your underlying belief systems, you can improve the way you feel.

Thought Reframing Log

Negative self-talk is likely something you have been engaging in for a long time, so changing it might be easier said than done. It takes effort to change a bad habit, but the good news is that scientific research shows that we can actually change the neurochemistry of our brains by practicing new ways of thinking.

The steps involved in changing your thinking are as follows:

1. Pay attention to the emotions you are experiencing.
2. When you notice yourself experiencing a strong emotion, stop and consider what thoughts are contributing to how you are feeling.
3. Write these thoughts down in sentence form.
4. Identify any negative, distorted, or irrational thinking.
5. Reframe the thought into something more neutral, rational, or encouraging.

Try it now. Notice how you are feeling and pinpoint what you are thinking. Writing the thought down on paper will help you put it into sentence form, and from there you can work to identify any distorted thinking and reframe it into a more effective message.

For example, if you found yourself feeling bad and thinking, "I'm such a loser," stop and change this sentence into something more neutral. Your reframed thought doesn't have to be the extreme opposite. You don't have to think, "I'm so cool. I'm so smart." Instead it could be something neutral and rational like, "Everyone makes mistakes" or "We all have moments of weakness." Use the following chart to track your negative self-talk:

EMOTION	THOUGHT	REFRAME
Upset	I'm such a loser.	Everyone makes mistakes.

The more you practice catching and reframing distorted thinking, the better you will become at preventing the negative self-talk that destroys self-esteem. Continue using the log for any negative thoughts you have this week.

Thought-Stopping Visual

Some people find it helpful to use a visual aid to imagine physically stopping the negative thoughts every time they notice them. For example, any time you catch yourself thinking in self-critical ways, imagine a big red stop sign or a slamming door—or be creative and come up with your own imagery!

Draw the visual aid you plan to use here:

Stopping Should-ing Yourself

Another form of distorted thinking that sets us up for failure is the tendency to think in rigid ways, using "should" statements. Should statements include any messages that start with things like "I should," "I should not," "I must," and "I have to." Should statements cause feelings of anger, guilt, frustration, and resentment because of the strict and unbending expectations they create. They set us up to feel bad about ourselves because when we don't meet the criteria behind the "should" statement, we wind up feeling like a failure.

Think of some "should" statements that show up in your thinking and write them in the space below. For example, *"I should get perfect grades," "I should be more outgoing," "I must make it to every practice," and "I have to be the perfect child."*

_____

_____

_____

_____

Look back over your "should" statements and determine what might happen if you do not meet the expectations set behind them. What's the worst that could happen?

_____

_____

_____

_____

When you consider the worst that could happen, do your responses seem trivial or critical? Either way, the thought of not living up to the expectations in the "should" statements likely creates some feelings of anxiety and even resistance. These things get in the way of completing tasks to the best of your ability. "Should" statements create problems because they don't leave room for error or unforeseeable circumstances that might get in the way.

Tackling "should" statements involves reframing the message to use language that is less rigid. By giving your sentences and directives more flexibility, you build in some padding to allow for things to potentially go wrong. And when they do, you're less likely to personalize the setbacks. Below are examples of "should" substitutions:

Should Substitutes

Instead of	Substitute
"I should"	"I could"
"I must"	"I'd like to"
"I have to"	"I choose to"
"I need to"	"I want to"

Using the substitution words above, try rewriting five of your own "should" statements.

"SHOULD" STATEMENTS	REFRAME
1.	
2.	
3.	
4.	
5.	

Substituting "Should"

Reflect on what happens when you change your should statements. Do you notice any differences in your body, like a change in your level of tension? Do you experience a shift in your anxiety or resistance level? Write about your observations here:

_____

_____

_____

_____

_____

_____

During the course of the next week, try to avoid using "should" statements. If you catch any of them in your speech or thoughts, try reframing them using the substitution phrases. Observe what changes or emotions you experience as a result of using slightly altered language and write about your experience here:

_____

_____

_____

_____

_____

_____

People with low self-esteem usually have perfectionist tendencies, which is often the reason behind many forms of negative self-talk. Perfectionism occurs when you constantly focus on what you didn't accomplish and your weaknesses rather than recognizing what you did well. Perfectionists strive to be perfect with the false belief that perfection and a lack of mistakes will improve their worth and self-esteem, but this approach ultimately backfires. Perfection is unrealistic and sets you up to feel bad about yourself.

To find out how much perfectionism might be getting in the way of your ability to have healthy self-esteem, take the following quiz:

Perfectionism Quiz

On a scale of 1 (not at all) to 5 (all the time), rate how often you engage in the following behaviors:

1. I focus on my failures more than my accomplishments.
   1   2   3   4   5

2. I notice my weaknesses more than my strengths.
   1   2   3   4   5

3. I set rigid standards for myself.
   1   2   3   4   5

4. I have difficulty making decisions.
   1   2   3   4   5

5. I tend to seek the approval of others.
   1   2   3   4   5

6. I rarely feel satisfied with myself or my performance.
   1   2   3   4   5

7. I struggle with procrastination.
   1   2   3   4   5

8. I place very strong demands on myself.
   1   2   3   4   5

9. I am very bothered by mistakes.
   1   2   3   4   5

10. I become defensive when criticized.
    1   2   3   4   5

Add up your score using the following point system:

1 point for every time you marked 1 (not at all)

2 points for every time you marked 2 (rarely)

3 points for every time you marked 3 (sometimes)

4 points for every time you marked 4 (often)

5 points for every time you marked 5 (all the time)

If you scored anywhere between 35 and 50, it's safe to say you're a perfectionist and that it'll be important for you to consider how it gets in the way of building your self-esteem. If you scored between 20 and 35, you may have a more rational view of yourself, but perfectionist tendencies still occasionally get in your way and you can also benefit from watching out for them. Scoring between 10 and 20 is very rare for somebody with low self-esteem and could indicate issues with denial or a lack of self-awareness.

What are your thoughts and observations regarding how you scored?

_____

_____

_____

Preventing Perfectionism

Improving self-esteem involves letting go of the need to be perfect and accepting that perfectionism is an unrealistic goal. As you work to lower the pressure you put on yourself, consider the following questions:

What would it take for me to lower my standards of myself just a little?

_____

_____

_____

What might happen if I accept my imperfections?

_____

_____

_____

What's the worst thing that could happen if I allow myself to be less than perfect or to accept mistakes?

_____

_____

_____

What are the differences between being perfect and trying my best?

_____

_____

_____

What are some goals I can set around giving myself some slack and letting go of the tendency to strive for perfection?

_____

_____

_____

CREATING AFFIRMATIONS

As I mentioned previously, it's possible to rewire your brain to think more positively, which can help you feel better and develop healthy self-esteem. But we can't rewire our brains by just reframing negatives. We also need to regularly use positive, self-encouraging messages. These are referred to as affirmations.

Think of your self-esteem as being held in a Styrofoam cup. Imagine that every time you engage in negative self-talk, it's like poking a hole in your cup and letting your self-esteem drain out. Affirmations are like filling those holes back up. But because negative statements tend to have more weight than positive ones, research shows that it's not enough to just fill those holes back up. We need to arm ourselves with at least five positive statements to counterbalance every negative one. Given how often you likely engage in negative self-talk, that means you will need *a lot* of affirmations to tip the scale toward feeling more optimistic and positive about yourself.

Affirmations 101

Affirmations are short, simple statements that convey a positive or encouraging message. They are most effective when written in the present tense, which gives them more power. Below is a list of affirmations that will aid in building your self-esteem. Read them over on a daily basis. Highlight the ones that feel the most unbelievable, as these will be the ones you need to practice the most.

I love myself.

I believe in myself.

I accept my imperfect self.

I deserve love and respect.

I know I am worthy.

I am unique and wonderful.

You might not 100% believe in these affirmations, but that's okay. Say them anyway. Sometimes you need to "fake it 'til you make it," but eventually you will begin to believe these statements.

My Personal Affirmations

Now come up with your own list of 10 more affirmations. They can include positive things you already believe about yourself or things you are working toward. If you get stuck, search "affirmations" on Google for inspiration.

_____

_____

_____

_____

_____

If writing and saying positive statements to yourself is really hard, start by using a bridge phrase, such as "I am learning to." For example, "I am learning to love myself."

Now rewrite your list of affirmations on a separate piece of paper. Hang them in your room or carry them with you, making sure to read them over every day.

Adolescence is a time to explore and become comfortable with your own identity. But sometimes you might wander down a path that causes you to lose sight of who you truly are. Let's take some time now to get back in touch with the real you.

All About Me

When your self-esteem is low, it can be difficult to identify seemingly basic things, such as what you like. You might look to others to guide your preferences or become so depressed that thinking about positive things is difficult. Part of building self-esteem involves remembering your own likes and dislikes.

Take a moment to answer the following questions:

My favorite color is _____

My favorite food is _____

My favorite place is _____

My favorite activity is _____

My favorite hobby or interest is _____

My favorite class or subject is _____

My least favorite thing to do is _____

My least favorite class or subject is _____

My favorite show, movie, or book is _____

My favorite music or song is _____

When I have alone time, I like to _____

If I could choose anywhere to go, it would be _____

As a child, when I grew up, I wanted to be _____

My dream job would be _____

If I could have dinner with anyone, I would choose _____

One of my favorite memories is _____

One of my greatest accomplishments is _____

One of my greatest challenges has been _____

A defining moment in my life so far has been _____

If you found it difficult to answer any of the questions above, think about what got in the way. Make a concentrated effort to get to know yourself again and explore what you like and what you don't like. Watch out for the tendency to follow others or to engage in negative self-talk that judges what you enjoy. Healthy self-esteem involves being able to own your preferences.

Consider Your Strengths

People with healthy self-esteem are able to honor their strengths and take pride in their accomplishments. Take a moment now to list at least three things in each of the boxes below:

MY POSITIVE QUALITIES	MY TALENTS	MY ACHIEVEMENTS

If you found it hard to fill the boxes, think about why. Do you have a hard time acknowledging your strengths due to low self-esteem? Or do you fear appearing boastful or conceited? Remember, healthy self-esteem and the ability to recognize your strengths are not the same as arrogance. As you move forward, try to find the courage to celebrate your strengths.

Evaluating Beliefs and Values

In Part One, we talked about the definition of self-esteem as it applies to teenagers. As you may recall, part of the definition of self-esteem involves demonstrating self-respect and adhering to your own values. So let's take some time to consider what your personal beliefs and values are and where they come from.

Personal beliefs and values can stem from many things—the way you were raised, the things you witnessed as a child, or the interpretations you made based on how you were treated. Sometimes the foundations of values and belief systems are influenced by religious or cultural aspects. Adolescence is a time when you start evaluating your own personal beliefs and start making your own choices about how you want to be and what you are willing to tolerate from others.

Values Checklist

Next is a list of common values. Check the ones that are important to you. Think about what you have learned about each value and how you demonstrate—or fail to demonstrate—these values today. Write about your thoughts and observations in the corresponding columns.

VALUE	WHAT HAVE I LEARNED ABOUT THIS VALUE?	DO I ADHERE TO THIS VALUE IN TERMS OF HOW I TREAT AND EXPECT TO BE TREATED BY OTHERS?
☐ Kindness		
☐ Compassion		
☐ Acceptance		
☐ Honesty		
☐ Trustworthiness		
☐ Loyalty		
☐ Patience		

VALUE	WHAT HAVE I LEARNED ABOUT THIS VALUE?	DO I ADHERE TO THIS VALUE IN TERMS OF HOW I TREAT AND EXPECT TO BE TREATED BY OTHERS?
☐ Fairness		
☐ Authenticity		
☐ Humility		
☐ Peace		
☐ Balance		
☐ Determination		
☐ Openness		
☐ Optimism		
☐ Happiness		
☐ Hard work		

Values Considerations

Think about where your personal values come from. What has been the biggest influence?

_____

_____

_____

_____

Has your value system been impacted in any way by distorted thinking or dysfunctional messages from your past? If so, reflect on that here:

_____

_____

_____

_____

Are you honoring the values that are important to you, or are there any improvements you need to make to better align with what you believe in? Write about your thoughts here:

_____

_____

_____

_____

Gender and Sexual Preference Check-In

For some, one of the biggest challenges during adolescence may be coming to terms with gender and sexuality. As a teen in today's world, you may view gender as being a spectrum. You probably understand that gender identity and sexual preference are not the same thing. And you might feel frustrated that older generations don't really understand or differentiate these issues.

The fact is, the world today is talking about gender in a much different way than in previous decades. Diversity in sexual preference is better tolerated but still often stigmatized. Put aside any frustration around society's standards and the judgments of others for a moment and focus solely on your own experience as you answer the following questions:

Regarding gender, how do you currently identify and what pronouns do you prefer?

If you have experienced any confusion or uncertainty about your gender identify, write about your struggles below:

Whether you identify as cisgender or transgender, how does growing up in an era where gender identity is viewed by some to be on a spectrum impact your sense of self?

_____

_____

_____

_____

_____

In terms of sexual preference, how do you identify?

_____

_____

_____

_____

_____

Has your sexual preference impacted your self-esteem in any way? If so, write about it here:

_____

_____

_____

_____

_____

If you have faced challenges regarding gender identity and/or sexual preference and feeling accepted, what steps can you take to feel more confident?

_____

_____

_____

_____

_____

What needs to happen in order for you to feel okay with who you are?

_____

_____

_____

_____

_____

Regarding your previous answers, what do you have control over?

_____

_____

_____

_____

_____

LGBTQ Support

If you identify as something other than gender binary and heterosexual, pay particular attention to how your experience has impacted your feelings of self-worth. Coming out can be a huge challenge for teens, and the reactions of family and friends can make or break the experience. If you are coming out and are struggling without adequate support, please see the resources at the end of this book and remember that your worth is not determined by the opinions of others.

Knowing My Needs

People with healthy self-esteem recognize that their needs are valid and just as important as those of anyone else. They recognize that they have the right to ask for what they need and want. Think about what your needs are and whether they are currently being met. Perhaps you need extra help in a certain subject. Maybe you feel a need for more space from your siblings. Are there things you wish for but don't feel you can ask for? Watch out for the tendency to reject your own needs due to self-talk that says you are undeserving or unimportant.

Write about any of your unmet needs here:

_____

_____

_____

_____

_____

_____

Consider why these needs are not currently being met. Do you have a hard time asking for help? Or have you found that others do not respect your requests?

_____

_____

_____

_____

_____

Do you have any distorted self-talk messages that tell you your needs are not valid and important?

_____

_____

_____

_____

_____

What could you do differently to have a better chance at having your needs met?

_____

_____

_____

_____

_____

PEOPLE-PLEASING PROBLEMS

People with low self-esteem tend to be people pleasers. They give away their power, allowing others to control them, and they rely on everyone but themselves to call all the shots. This may be due to distorted beliefs around your needs not being important or the desire to gain the approval of others. Either way, putting your own needs on the back burner in order to please everyone else ultimately destroys self-esteem—and leads to resentment and burnout.

People-Pleasing Questionnaire

Take the following questionnaire to find out if you are a people pleaser:

On a scale of 1 (not at all) to 5 (all the time), rate how often you engage in the following behaviors:

1. I say "yes" when I want to say "no."

   1   2   3   4   5

2. I take on responsibilities even when I don't really want to.

   1   2   3   4   5

3. I feel I have to profusely apologize or make excuses when I can't say "yes" to someone.

   1   2   3   4   5

4. I feel responsible for other people's feelings.

   1   2   3   4   5

5. I keep my thoughts and opinions to myself if they're different from those of others.

   1   2   3   4   5

6. I feel very upset if someone is mad at me or doesn't like me.

   1   2   3   4   5

7. I have a hard time admitting to others that they have hurt my feelings or upset me.

   1   2   3   4   5

8. I go to great lengths to avoid conflict.

   1   2   3   4   5

Add up your score using the following point system:

1 point for every time you marked 1 (not at all)

2 points for every time you marked 2 (rarely)

3 points for every time you marked 3 (sometimes)

4 points for every time you marked 4 (often)

5 points for every time you marked 5 (all the time)

If you scored above 20 points, you likely struggle with people-pleasing. You will benefit from dedicating time and effort to recognize your own needs and taking time for yourself.

Write about what makes it difficult to make yourself a priority:

_____

_____

_____

_____

_____

_____

_____

_____

What are three ways you can challenge these beliefs?

1. _____

2. _____

3. _____

ATTENTION TO APPEARANCE

Your appearance is one of the first things people notice when meeting you. It can convey information about who you are. Some aspects of appearance, such as body shape and facial features, are out of our control. Others, like how we dress or style our hair, can be altered based on our preferences. The thoughts we have about our own appearance and the way we interpret the feedback we receive from others about it can impact self-esteem.

How do you feel about your own appearance?

_____

_____

_____

_____

_____

What aspects of your appearance do you appreciate and feel good about?

_____

_____

_____

_____

_____

What aspects of your appearance make you feel insecure?

_____

_____

_____

_____

_____

What feedback—positive or negative—have you received from others regarding your appearance and how you dress?

_____

_____

_____

_____

_____

How do these comments impact your self-esteem?

_____

_____

_____

_____

_____

Studying Your Style

Another challenge in adolescence is keeping up with the latest styles and trends, which constantly change. It can be hard to figure out how to look and what to wear in order to fit in versus stand out. The jeans that were super cool last year might be the dorkiest look ever now! And the hairstyle you thought was awesome last semester might raise eyebrows today.

Think about your own style and how you tend to dress.

What style choices have you made that you feel good about?

_____

_____

What style choices have you regretted?

_____

_____

What factors typically motivate what you wear? Check any that apply.
- ☐ I like to keep up with the latest fashion.
- ☐ I like to dress for comfort.
- ☐ I don't really care how I look.
- ☐ I put a lot of effort into deciding how I look and what to wear.
- ☐ I like to blend in with everyone else.
- ☐ I enjoy standing out and being noticed.
- ☐ I use fashion and style to express who I am.
- ☐ Fashion and style are not that important to me.

If you tend to feel insecure about your choices in style and appearance, make a point to say the following affirmation every morning when you get dressed:

"I'm proud to be me. I enjoy expressing myself the way I want to. Opinions of others are just that—their opinions. My own opinion of myself is what matters, and I'm learning to love who I am."

Body Image Inventory

When self-esteem is low, it can be especially challenging to maintain a healthy body image. We often judge our bodies harshly, succumbing to perfectionism and unrealistic ideals that reinforce low self-esteem. Part of building self-esteem involves learning to appreciate your body and to refrain from dwelling on physical shortcomings and flaws.

Let's take a look at how you judge your own body. In the space below, draw a sketch of yourself and pinpoint the areas you focus on most. Highlight anything you really appreciate about your body and note anything that really bothers you.

Now on a separate piece of paper, ask a friend, family member, significant other, or someone who really loves and cares about you to draw a sketch of you, pointing out any of your most notable physical traits.

Compare the two illustrations. Write about what you notice in terms of similarities and differences.

_____

_____

_____

_____

_____

People with low self-esteem are more prone to focus on, obsess over, and beat themselves up for negative physical traits. But doing so just reinforces low self-esteem. It's okay to have goals regarding how you want to look and the body type you'd ideally like to have, but make sure these goals are realistic and obtainable, and aren't perfectionist standards.

Choose at least one positive trait from one of the illustrations and create an affirmation that celebrates it, then read this affirmation on a daily basis.

_____

_____

_____

_____

_____

_____

Stopping Destructive Body Shaming

Consider how distorted thinking plays a role in your own opinion of your body image and appearance. Do you hold any negative or rigid beliefs about how you *should* look or how life might be better if your appearance somehow changed?

_____

_____

_____

_____

_____

Choose an affirmation below that you will commit to repeating any time you find yourself beating yourself up over body image issues:

- ☐ I appreciate all that my body does.
- ☐ I am unique and beautiful just the way I am.
- ☐ My body deserves my respect.
- ☐ I am learning to appreciate my body and image.

Write your affirmation down on a sticky note. Place it on your bathroom mirror and remember to read the affirmation out loud every day when you brush your teeth.

FAMILY FACTORS

The verbal and nonverbal messages that we receive from our family play a role in shaping our level of self-esteem. From a very early age—before we can even speak—we are observing others and trying to make sense of the way those around us treat us.

Consider your role in your family and where you fall in the birth order if you have siblings. How do these factors impact the messages you received? How do your family members treat you?

Messages Checklist

Look over the following list and check any messages that resonate with you.

In my family I was/am:

☐ Liked	☐ Disliked
☐ Unconditionally loved	☐ Unloved or loved conditionally
☐ Wanted	☐ Unwanted
☐ Appreciated	☐ Unappreciated or underappreciated
☐ Trusted	☐ Doubted, suspected, or disbelieved
☐ Valued	☐ Rejected
☐ Cared for physically	☐ Neglected physically
☐ Cared for emotionally	☐ Neglected emotionally
☐ Protected	☐ Ignored or abandoned
☐ Smart	☐ Stupid
☐ Good	☐ Bad
☐ Giving	☐ Selfish
☐ A priority	☐ A burden or a nuisance
☐ Free to be independent	☐ An object to make others happy
☐ Able to make mistakes	☐ Expected to be perfect
☐ Able to show feelings	☐ Expected to hide my feelings
☐ Attractive	☐ Unattractive
☐ Happy	☐ Sad
☐ Acceptable	☐ Flawed and inadequate
☐ Successful	☐ A failure
☐ Important	☐ Unimportant
☐ A source of pride	☐ A disappointment or embarrassment
☐ Capable	☐ Incompetent
☐ Labeled as delightful	☐ Labeled as a troublemaker

Know that it's completely normal to check seemingly conflicting messages. Often, we receive mixed messages or different messages from different people. For example, imagine that one parent consistently says, "I love you," but that same parent—or the other—never shows up for significant events, leaving you to question your own value and worth.

Which items that you checked seem to have the most impact on your self-esteem?

_____

_____

_____

_____

_____

_____

_____

Dysfunction in Families

Low self-esteem is often a consequence of growing up in a family where there is any form of dysfunction. Consider what family dynamics may have contributed to how you view your own sense of worth. Check any factors that apply to your experience.

In my family, there was/is:

☐ Abuse

☐ Addiction

☐ Frequent angry outbursts

☐ Poor communication

☐ Lack of emotional expression

☐ Criticism

☐ Hostile sarcasm

☐ Unclear expectations

☐ Toxic secrets

Reflect on how these experiences impacted you:

_____

_____

_____

_____

Exploring My Childhood Experience

As you think more about your history, the experiences you've encountered, and the messages you received in childhood, complete the following sentences:

Growing up, I've felt:

_____

_____

_____

_____

My parents and caretakers are:

_____

_____

_____

_____

My relationships with my siblings are:

_____

_____

_____

_____

The best aspects of my childhood were:

_____

_____

_____

_____

The worst parts of my childhood were:

_____

_____

_____

_____

It's not just your family that can impact your development of self-esteem. Anyone in your network can impact it negatively or positively. Remember, you can't improve self-esteem by gaining acceptance and approval from external sources, but how you *think* about the way others perceive and treat you largely impacts your sense of self.

Knowing My Network

Identify the significant figures in your life from the past and present and add them to the circles below. Put the closest relationships at the center and the more distant but influential relationships toward the outer circles. Think about extended family, mentors, teachers, coaches, friends, neighbors, supportive groups, and organizations you are part of. Star the connections that had a positive impact on your self-esteem, and circle the ones that negatively impacted your sense of self.

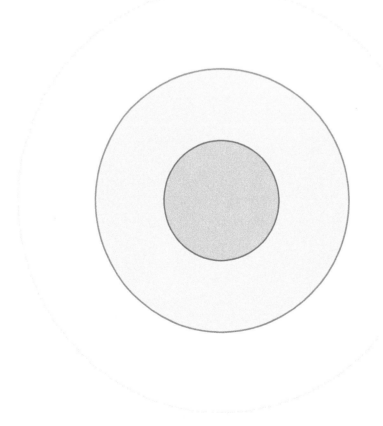

Consider how each of these relationships may have contributed to your current level of self-esteem:

_____

_____

_____

_____

_____

Which relationships were impactful in terms of helping you feel worthy? How so?

_____

_____

_____

_____

If any of these relationships negatively impact your development of healthy self-esteem, reflect on them here:

_____

_____

_____

_____

Negative Experiences Checklist

Some kids have the unfortunate experience of struggling with negative social encounters that cause a lot of pain and destroy their self-esteem. Have you faced any of the below experiences?

- ☐ Bullying
- ☐ Abuse (physical, emotional, sexual)
- ☐ Frequent criticism
- ☐ Ridicule
- ☐ Exclusion
- ☐ Peer pressure

If you checked anything on the list above, reflect on how these experiences impacted your self-esteem:

_____

_____

_____

_____

_____

What are some ways you can move past these experiences?

_____

_____

_____

_____

_____

Monitoring Society's Messages

Self-esteem can be challenged by the interpretations and comparisons we make regarding what we see in the media and advertising. It's important to be aware that what we see isn't always real or obtainable. For example, recognize that the models in most ads are digitally altered to appear perfect—their skin is airbrushed, body parts are slimmed, colors are changed, and shading is applied. And sometimes what you see is actually the composition of multiple different people!

Pay attention to what you come across in the media this week. Choose five different ads—on TV, in magazines, on billboards, or on social media—and fill in the chart below:

	DESCRIBE THE AD. WHAT IS IT FOR? WHAT IS THE TONE?	WHAT DO YOU NOTICE ABOUT THE APPEARANCE OF THE PEOPLE?	HOW DOES THIS AD MAKE YOU FEEL ABOUT YOURSELF?	HOW MIGHT THIS AD IMPACT YOUR SELF-ESTEEM?
1.				
2.				
3.				
4.				
5.				

Developing greater awareness regarding the superficial nature of media can help you protect your self-esteem. Watch for any distorted thinking that tells you things like, "If I looked like that model, my life would be better" or "If only I could be that flawless."

Note any negative thinking you experience that relates to what you see in the media.

Create three affirmations that can be used to reduce the impact that society's messages could have on your self-esteem:

1. _____

2. _____

3. _____

Monitoring Your Social Media

Being a teen in today's world means you are probably well versed in social media. Social media can be a great tool to connect people and keep up-to-date with family and friends. But it can also create a number of challenges, especially when you are constantly seeing images that lead you to make assumptions and comparisons that pose a threat to healthy self-esteem.

Make a list of all your social media accounts:

_____

_____

_____

_____

_____

_____

_____

Now spend a few minutes looking at the feeds and updates on each of your social media accounts. Write about what you observe and any emotions you feel.

_____

_____

_____

_____

_____

Have you ever felt tempted to delete your accounts? If so, why?

_____

_____

_____

_____

_____

If you have deleted accounts, what did it accomplish? Was it hard to stop using social media? Why or why not?

_____

_____

_____

_____

_____

What benefits do you get from using social media?

_____

_____

_____

_____

_____

What are the negatives or drawbacks of using social media?

_____

_____

_____

_____

_____

Weighing Social Media's Pros and Cons

Monitor your social media use over the next week and try to identify approximately how many hours you spend engaged in it. Using tick marks on the scale below, track how often you feel happy and fulfilled by the images you see and the conversations you have versus how often you feel sad, overwhelmed, anxious, or burdened.

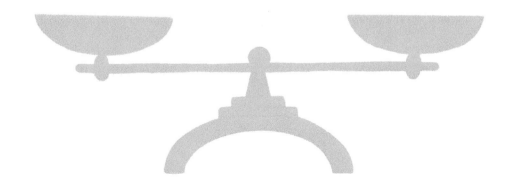

NEGATIVE EXPERIENCES WITH SOCIAL MEDIA

POSITIVE EXPERIENCES WITH SOCIAL MEDIA

After tracking your social media use for a week or so, write about what you notice about the positives or negatives about social media:

_____

_____

_____

_____

_____

If you did experience negatives, what goals can you set to limit your usage or to change how you use social media?

_____

_____

_____

_____

_____

IDENTIFYING YOUR STRESSORS

Everyone experiences stress, and some levels of stress are actually useful because they can make us alert and create the motivation necessary to get things done. But we all have a threshold for how much stress we can manage before we become completely overwhelmed.

Imagine every stressor—every responsibility, role, problem, and hassle in your life—to be like a brick. When you have one or two bricks piled up, it's not all that heavy, and life feels manageable. But as those bricks start to pile higher and higher, you reach your stress threshold and eventually feel crushed by all the pressure.

Take a few minutes to identify all the stressors in your life. Consider both major ones—an upcoming test, a move, a family member's illness—as well as minor ones—bad traffic on your commute to school, forgetting your lunch money. Also include all your roles in life—child, sibling, student, friend—as well as every class and activity that is part of your week. Some of these things might not be considered a stressor individually, but they do come with expectations and responsibilities that contribute to all you have on your plate.

Write each stressor in a brick:

Sometimes visualizing our stressors in this way can help us understand why we feel so overwhelmed. Alone, each brick might not seem like that big of a challenge, but when we see the stressors piling up, it's easier to understand why coping can become difficult.

How does seeing all your stressors laid out impact you?

_____

_____

_____

_____

_____

_____

Create affirmations that can help you be mindful of your stressors. For example, *"I have a lot on my plate and am patient with myself."* Write affirmations on the write-on lines below.

_____

_____

_____

_____

_____

_____

Super Stressors

Adolescence is a time of taking on new things. You are pulled in more directions and have more responsibilities than ever before. Developing awareness of all the stressors you are juggling can help you give yourself a break and recognize that it's normal to feel overwhelmed at times.

Below are some major life stressors that teens can face. If any of these items apply to you, make sure you did not forget them in your stack of bricks. Know that these particular stressors bring about major challenges, so be patient with yourself as you find the self-compassion that will be necessary to handle your situation and build self-esteem:

☐ Single-parent family

☐ Divorce or separation of parents

☐ Death of a family member, friend, or pet

☐ Parent's loss of a job or changes in work/life balance

☐ Change in family's financial status

☐ Health concerns of self or a family member

☐ Addiction in family

☐ Dysfunction or abuse in family

☐ You or a family member questioning sexuality or coming out

☐ Moving to a new home

☐ Switching schools

☐ Failing classes

☐ Diagnosis of a learning disability, ADHD, etc.

ACTING ASSERTIVELY

One consequence of low self-esteem is that it can be very difficult to speak up, communicate your opinions, and ask for what you want. When self-esteem is low, we tell ourselves that our needs are not important, and we convince ourselves that speaking up will cause us to be judged unfavorably. As you work to challenge distorted messages that make it hard to stand up for yourself, you can begin developing assertiveness skills.

There are three ways of communicating when it comes to expressing feelings, opinions, boundaries, wants, and needs: (1) Passive communication happens when we avoid speaking up. (2) Aggressive communication happens when we let our frustration or resentment build to the point of blowing up. The goal is (3) assertive communication, where we speak up but do so in a calm and respectful manner.

Styles of Communication

Look at the following chart and see if you can pinpoint examples of times you have used each form of communication. Think about the reasons you utilized one style versus another. For times you acted in a manner that was passive or aggressive (or a combination of the two—passive-aggressive), what would it have taken for you to act more assertively? If there were times you were assertive, think about what enabled you to be that way and what the result was.

PASSIVE	ASSERTIVE	AGGRESSIVE
Doesn't speak up	Speaks up	Blows up
Submissive, weak, anxious	Self-assured, considerate	Domineering, hostile, mean
Lets others decide	Allows everyone to make own choices	Pushes own decisions on others
Disrespects self	Respects everyone	Disrespects others
Reinforces own low self-esteem	Maintains self-esteem	Destroys own and others' self-esteem

Assertiveness Scenarios

Read over the following scenarios and consider how you might respond. Then read the examples of passive, assertive, and aggressive responses and select which option seems most in line with how you imagined yourself responding.

1. Two friends are spending the night while your parents are out of town. They decide to invite others over and soon people start showing up, thinking you're hosting a party.

    How would you handle the situation?

    _____

    _____

2. A teacher asks you to stay after school to help with a project. You have other plans.

    What would you do?

    _____

    _____

3. A friend borrows your sweater and returns it with a stain.

    How do you react?

    _____

    _____

4. You're in line to buy snacks at an event. You have your back turned while you talk to a friend. When you turn around, you discover a group of other students have joined their friends and cut in front of you.

What would you do?

_____

_____

5. Your parents say "no" when you ask to go to beach week with friends.

How would you respond?

_____

_____

6. You overhear two classmates talking about how your best friend kissed your crush at a party last weekend.

What would you do?

_____

_____

Here are different ways of responding to each of the previous scenarios. Compare your responses and think about how likely you would be to act in line with the assertive way of handling each scenario.

1. Two friends start a party at your house:
   PASSIVE: Fearing looking uncool, you go along with the party, hoping nothing gets out of control and that you can clean up before your parents get back.
   ASSERTIVE: Tell your friends that you are upset they invited people over without your permission. Insist that they text everyone to let them know the plan is off and tell those who arrive that you're unable to let them in.
   AGGRESSIVE: Freak out and scream at your friends. Kick everyone out and threaten to call the cops.

2. Teacher wants you to help after school:
   PASSIVE: Say, "Sure. No problem," fearing that she'll be mad or think less of you if you don't agree to stay. Cancel your plans.
   ASSERTIVE: Tell her you'd be happy to help but have plans today and will need to schedule a time that works for you both.
   AGGRESSIVE: Get mad and say, "I have a life outside of school! You can't just expect me to be available 24/7!"

3. Sweater with a stain:
   PASSIVE: Spray the stain, hoping it comes out in the wash, and don't mention it to your friend.
   ASSERTIVE: Confront your friend in a calm manner, saying, "I noticed a stain on my sweater. Do you know what happened?"
   AGGRESSIVE: Text the friend, "WTF!? My sweater has a huge stain on the front!" and decide to never loan anything again.

4. Being cut in line:
   PASSIVE: Say nothing and suck up the fact that your wait time just significantly increased.
   ASSERTIVE: Interrupt their conversation, saying, "Sorry to interrupt, but the end of the line is back there."
   AGGRESSIVE: Loud enough for others to hear, say to your friend, "OMG! I can't believe these jerks cut in front of us!"

5. Beach week denied:

    PASSIVE: Pout and walk away without saying much, then text your friend group telling them it's not going to happen.

    ASSERTIVE: Say to your parents, "I understand you're saying no and I'm not challenging your decision, but could you help me to understand your concerns and reasons so I know *why* you are saying no?"

    AGGRESSIVE: Throw a fit, telling them they are the worst parents ever and that you can't wait to turn 18 and move out of the house.

6. Friend kissed your crush:

    PASSIVE: Try to act normal around your friend, pretending you don't know or care.

    ASSERTIVE: Address it with your friend, saying you overheard a rumor that hurt your feelings and you want to talk.

    AGGRESSIVE: Spread rumors about your friend being promiscuous.

What were your reactions to assertive versus passive or aggressive responses? If you find assertiveness to be a challenge, write about why:

_____

_____

_____

_____

What initial goals can you establish for developing assertiveness skills?

_____

_____

_____

_____

_____

HEALTHY COPING

In Part One, we discussed some of the unhealthy ways that teens tend to cope with their struggles, and you had the opportunity to begin pinpointing some of the unhealthy coping mechanisms you sometimes turn to. Now, let's think about some of the positive ways you deal with stress. Maybe you talk to friends, journal or blog, play video games to pass the time, or take yoga classes. Coping tools can be anything you do for enjoyment or managing stress. They are considered healthy when they cause no harm and are used in moderation.

My Coping Tools

In the box, list any tools or hobbies that you consider healthy distractions or positive ways of coping:

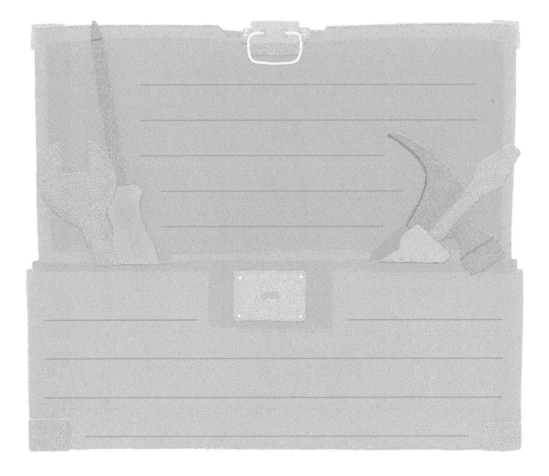

Evaluating My Coping Tools

Now look back over your list of coping skills and answer the following questions:

How many coping skills have you listed? _____

How often do you engage in each of these activities? _____

_____

_____

When do you tend to turn to each of these items? _____

_____

_____

When do you feel these coping tools are not enough? _____

_____

_____

If you listed 10 or more coping skills, good job! You have a nice list but will want to pay attention to how often you use these skills and how effective they really are. If you listed fewer than 10 activities, part of your work will be to fill this box up with more ways to cope with stress and negative emotions.

The goal is to have *many* tools in your coping skills box and include a wide variety of activities. Some days you will have the time and financial resources to devote to activities that are more involved, like taking a class, getting a massage, or going to an event. Other times you might have only five minutes to spare and will need something quick and easy to turn to.

Increasing Your Coping Tools

Make sure you have a wide variety of tools and pleasurable activities to choose from by adding new ideas to your coping skills box. It may take some trial and error to discover which items are helpful, but think of your box as something you can continuously add to or take things out of.

Brainstorm more ideas you can add to your box or choose some from the following list:

☐ Go for a walk	
☐ Watch a sunset	
☐ Watch a funny movie	
☐ Call a best friend	
☐ Take a hot shower	
☐ Take a nap	
☐ Play with a pet	
☐ Journal	
☐ Write a poem	
☐ Exercise	
☐ Play a game	
☐ Create a collage	
☐ Dance	
☐ Learn a new skill	
☐ Look up new jokes online	
☐ Volunteer	
☐ Visit a park	
☐ Email an old friend	
☐ Listen to favorite music (but beware of angry or depressing music, which can make you feel worse)	

Stop Sabotaging Self-Care

Self-care refers to anything we do to nurture or take good care of ourselves. It includes the basics, like eating well and getting enough rest. It also includes all the things we do to enjoy life and relax.

If you had a hard time filling your coping skills box in the previous exercise, or if you discovered you are not engaging in these activities on a regular basis, stop and think about why. Failure to engage in good self-care often stems from negative thinking and faulty beliefs. If you tend to put self-care on the back burner, consider whether any of the following statements contribute to the reasons why:

- ☐ I don't have time for self-care.
- ☐ I feel guilty when I take time out for myself.
- ☐ My needs are not as important as those of others.
- ☐ Taking time out for myself is not a priority.
- ☐ Taking time out for myself is selfish.
- ☐ Others will view my self-care activities as foolish.
- ☐ Engaging in self-care activities is a waste of time.
- ☐ Self-care activities are frivolous.

Are there any other reasons you neglect self-care?

_____

_____

_____

_____

_____

_____

_____

Lifestyle Considerations

Think about your current experiences with eating, sleeping, and exercise. If you are happy with how things are going in these areas, write a few notes about what is working well. If you are not happy in these areas, what realistic goals can you set to make changes and find a healthier balance?

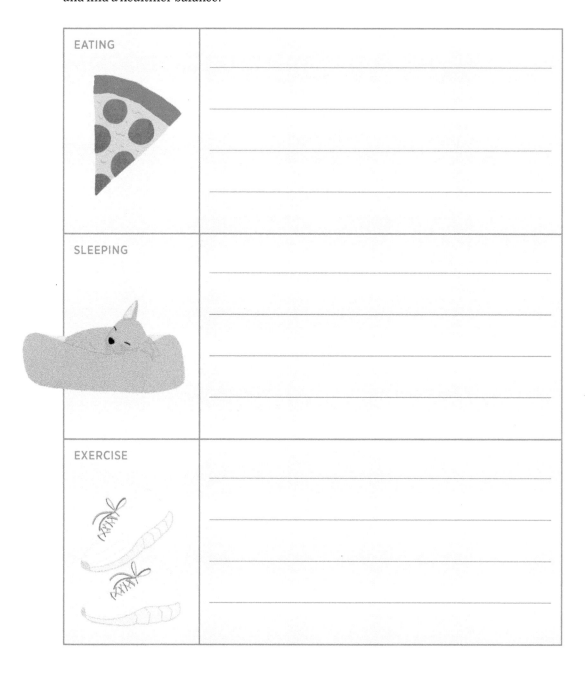

EATING

SLEEPING

EXERCISE

Embrace Mindfulness

Becoming more mindful is an important part of taking care of yourself, and there are tons of resources that can be used as coping tools. One simple way to be more mindful is to stop and focus on your five senses. Try it now:

1. Name three things you can see.

   _____

   _____

2. What do you hear?

   _____

   _____

3. What do you smell?

   _____

   _____

4. Are you noticing any tastes?

   _____

   _____

5. Touch something near you and describe the texture and the way it feels.

   _____

   _____

By stopping to become aware of what we are experiencing in the present moment, we can interrupt our stream of self-talk and establish a greater sense of stability.

Mindfulness activities are easy to do, yet many of us forget how important mindfulness is as we get wrapped up in our fast-paced lives. Taking the time to practice and develop mindfulness skills is a great way to develop a calmer state of mind.

There are tons of smartphone apps available to help with mindfulness. Some walk you through guided meditations, whereas others provide calming melodies that you can listen to as you focus on being still in the present moment. Try some of the following apps and select the ones you find most helpful. Keep notes on which you like and why, then commit to using these apps on a regular basis. You can find more resources by searching "mindfulness" or "meditation" in Google, YouTube, or an app store.

THE MINDFULNESS APP	
HEADSPACE	
CALM	
BUDDHIFY	
BREATHE2RELAX	
SLEEP MACHINE	

ILLUSTRATE YOUR EMOTIONS

People with healthy self-esteem are generally in touch with their emotions. They're able to identify their feelings and experience them without shame or embarrassment. This isn't always easy, especially for people who grew up in an environment where showing emotions seemed scary or forbidden. Some people internalized the message that showing emotions was weak or off-limits, but acknowledging them is an important part of self-care.

Next are 18 common emotions that all humans experience. Without overthinking, create an illustration or sketch that represents each of the emotions. There is no right or wrong, and you don't have to be a great artist. Just draw whatever pictures, symbols, or ideas come to mind.

HAPPINESS	CONTENTMENT	SADNESS
PAIN	ANGER	FEAR
JEALOUSY	GUILT	SHAME

IRRITATION	GRIEF	LONELINESS
INSECURITY	DISCOMFORT	GRATITUDE
EXCITEMENT	OVERWHELMED	HOPE

Go back and look over your drawings and consider what it was like for you to create an illustration for each emotion.

Were any emotions easier or harder for you? _____

Sometimes we store emotions in our bodies. Did you notice any physical sensations as you contemplated each feeling?

_____

_____

Feeling My Feelings

Now take a look at these emotions again and consider the last time you felt each one. Jot down a few words or sentences to identify the situation or experience.

HAPPINESS

CONTENTMENT

SADNESS

PAIN

ANGER

FEAR

_____

_____

JEALOUSY

_____

_____

GUILT

_____

_____

SHAME

_____

_____

IRRITATION

_____

_____

GRIEF

_____

_____

LONELINESS

_____

_____

INSECURITY

_____

_____

DISCOMFORT

_____

_____

GRATITUDE

_____

_____

EXCITEMENT

_____

_____

OVERWHELMED

_____

_____

_____

_____

_____

What do you notice about your experiences with various feelings? Are there any links between emotions that were harder to draw and those that were harder to find examples for?

_____

_____

_____

_____

_____

What are your self-talk messages regarding your ability to experience each of these emotions?

_____

_____

_____

_____

_____

My Experience with Emotions

Teenagers often get criticized for being "hormonal" or "moody," and it's unfortunate that there is a negative stereotype around emotional expression among teens. Adolescence is a time of hormonal changes, and it's very normal to experience a wide range of changing emotions. By recognizing, identifying, and experiencing emotions, you are allowing yourself to engage in the full human experience. If you were able to identify a recent time when you felt each of these emotions, give yourself credit for being in touch with your feelings. If you found it difficult to identify with any of these emotions, take some time to think about why that may be. Do you tend to bottle up emotions? Did you receive messages in your past—verbally or otherwise—that showing emotions was not okay? Write about your thoughts here:

FREE YOURSELF FROM GUILT AND SHAME

People with low self-esteem often suffer from chronic shame. Shame is related to the negative self-talk messages that we discussed such as, "I am wrong" and "I am bad." These personal beliefs create a shame spiral, leaving you feeling terrible about who you are. To build self-esteem, it's important to tackle feelings of shame, but first we must understand that shame is different from guilt.

Guilt is when you feel bad about something you did. Shame is about feeling bad about who you are. When you feel guilty, it's useful to acknowledge the remorse and find a way to deal with it, perhaps by apologizing, so you can move beyond it. Shame requires a deeper dive into exploring and healing feelings of self-hatred.

Spend some time thinking about guilt and shame.

Things I feel guilty about are:

_____

_____

_____

_____

Steps I can take to move on:

_____

_____

_____

_____

Reasons I feel shame or embarrassment about who I am:

_____

_____

_____

_____

_____

If you struggle with shame, create three affirmations that will help you release these toxic feelings by accepting your imperfections:

1. _____

2. _____

3. _____

For a more in-depth look at understanding and tackling shame, watch Brené Brown's TED Talks on shame and vulnerability on YouTube.

FORGIVENESS AND LESSONS LEARNED

Write a letter of forgiveness to yourself in order to let go of guilt and feelings of shame. Imagine what you would say to a close friend in a similar situation. We often show more compassion to others than we do to ourselves. Use this as an opportunity to show yourself the same level of kindness and empathy. Consider whether you have learned any valuable lessons or discovered any silver linings amid your experiences. Remind yourself that you are human and mistakes are how we learn and grow.

Dear Self,

PART THREE

Overcoming Low Self-Esteem in Real Life

Hopefully you have taken some time to work through the exercises in Part Two and are now using some new tools to work toward better self-care and improved self-esteem. Regardless of where your self-esteem falls, you will encounter numerous challenges throughout life that force you to face uncertainty and difficult decisions.

Following are a number of questions and concerns voiced by teenagers dealing with various situations they encountered during adolescence. As you read over each question or concern, contemplate how your own experiences may overlap with the struggles these teens face. You may be dealing with similar scenarios or others that aren't covered here. Either way, consider whether you can apply any of the tips and advice to your own life as you continue to strive for healthy self-esteem.

"I hate going to school. I don't like any of the people there, and it's literally miserable every single day."

One of the most frustrating parts of being a teen is that you're becoming more independent, but you're still a minor and can't always make your own decisions. You have to follow rules and laws, and that usually means you have to attend school. If you are in a situation where you absolutely hate your school and feel isolated every day, you probably feel pretty miserable.

Some teens may have the opportunity to explore other options, like transferring schools or taking some of their classes online. Talk to your family and school counselor to see whether there are options that might work for you. If not, the unfortunate reality is that you may just have to suck it up and get through the next one to four years. I promise you, though: Life won't always seem this bleak. I've worked with so many teens who hated their high school years for various reasons, and I've been so thrilled to hear from many of them who reported loving college, where they thrived, found awesome friends, and had a blast.

College is so different from high school. You have way more freedom to choose classes you enjoy, set your schedule, and meet new people. It gives you a chance to have a fresh start with a clean slate where you can reinvent who you want to be. I encourage you to see the light at the end of the tunnel. You don't have to stay this unhappy forever, but you do have to find the energy to keep going. Otherwise you run the risk of getting swallowed up by the misery and sinking into a depression that makes everything harder.

If you hate your high school and the people you are surrounded by, try to make at least one friend so you don't feel so alone. Consider getting involved in some type of club or extracurricular activity, perhaps outside of your school where you can meet different people. Be very mindful of your self-talk. The more you think, "This is horrible and I can't stand it," the worse you will feel. Use affirmations, such as, "I can get through this" and "This won't last forever" to encourage yourself.

"A bunch of my friends have started going to parties on the weekends. Every time they invite me, I feel filled with anxiety. I worry about what to wear, how I look, how to act, and how to handle myself if people are doing things I don't want to do. It's hard for me to have fun when every second is filled with fear of whether or not I'll fit in. How do I learn to just enjoy myself without second-guessing every single thing?"

Social anxiety and low self-esteem often go hand in hand. When you lack confidence in who you are, your self-talk will likely be filled with constant anxious thoughts about whether you are doing the "right" things and being judged. The more you practice the tools in this book, the more you will begin to build self-esteem and learn to feel comfortable with being yourself and caring less about everyone else's opinions.

Continue to practice monitoring your negative and anxious self-talk, stopping all unhelpful messages in their tracks, and replacing them with more rational and self-serving sentences, such as, "No matter what, I will be okay" and "I can be myself and have a good time." Use affirmations such as, "I allow myself to relax and have fun" and "I'm okay being me." Watch out for the tendency to beat yourself up over things you perceive as mistakes or failures. Embrace the ability to laugh at yourself in a lighthearted manner and move past moments of feeling stupid. Challenge yourself to step outside your comfort zone and practice these techniques in social settings. The more you do so, the more you will build self-esteem and work toward decreasing social anxiety.

"I've recently gained weight and I feel disgusting. Yesterday I complained to my mom about how horrible I look and she told me I should stop using creamer in my coffee! Obviously she agrees I'm fat. In the past, she would always monitor what I ate and sometimes she gets on my case about exercising. I feel like how I look is all that matters!"

There can be nothing worse than sharing how bad you feel about yourself only to be met with a response that seems to reaffirm your self-doubts. This type of unsolicited advice comes across as condescending and judgmental when it's not accompanied by more compassionate words of support. Unfortunately, the people who care about us the most are often culprits of hurting our feelings because their desire to help—and their pain at seeing us suffer—gets in the way of their ability to reply in the most supportive and helpful manner.

When we feel upset about something and share it with others, we are seeking validation or hoping the person we are speaking to will alleviate our fears by saying something like, "You are not fat, honey!" Or maybe even just, "I'm so sorry! I know how much it sucks to feel unhappy with your weight." It might help to step outside your own hurt to look at the bigger picture and consider where your mother's comments stem from: Are her tips and advice attempts to help you solve your problem? Do they come from her personal experiences with weight struggles? Perhaps she's been made fun of in the past and wants to protect you from that hurt, or maybe she had parents who were overly critical of her appearance and is repeating what she learned.

Consider having an honest conversation with your mom to figure out how she really feels about your appearance and the role it plays in your life. As much as we are dealing with our own distorted thinking and internal critics, so is everyone else. Distorted thinking and dysfunctional patterns are often passed down through many generations, and it can be helpful to consider other people's belief systems and where they stem from.

There will always be people in our lives who miss the mark when it comes to offering support. But you can use your own positive self-talk to let their comments roll off your back rather than hurt you more. Sometimes it's helpful to use a visual aid to assist with this. Think of an air filter: Its job is to prevent debris, dirt, and dust from entering the air you breathe. Visualize having an imaginary filter in front of you and allow it to trap any hurtful or unconstructive comments, preventing them from impacting your self-esteem. If you are unhappy with an aspect of your appearance, instead of fixating on it or complaining to others who make you feel worse, put your energy into setting healthy goals relating to your appearance and working to feel comfortable in your own skin through loving affirmations.

"I'm really struggling with my family. Most of my life, my dad has been really distant, and we haven't gotten along. He was always a heavy drinker, and when he was drunk, he was nasty and cold. Recently he began attending a rehab program and got sober. Now everyone in my family is acting like he's the greatest thing in the world. My siblings can't understand why I'm not embracing him, but I just don't feel a sense of connection. I'm still so angry at all the times he's let me down. Am I a bad person for finding it hard to give him another chance?"

It's really challenging when people want you to move on or make changes before you are ready. The pressure can cause you to doubt yourself and question whether you are somehow doing things wrong. But healing from the wounds and trauma of the past takes time, and the journey will look different for each person. If you find yourself trapped by upsetting memories from the past or overwhelmed by complicated emotions, consider getting into therapy with an eye movement desensitization and reprocessing (EMDR) therapist (see the resources at the end of the book). EMDR is a powerful therapy tool that can help you process and resolve the emotional distress associated with upsetting life experiences.

There is no set time frame for healing, acceptance, or forgiveness to occur. Anytime there is dysfunction in a family—be it addiction, abuse, instability, chaos, or poor communication—it impacts your core being and can create patterns and belief systems that complicate your ability to navigate the world from a place of ease. In these types of complicated family situations, it's helpful to acknowledge that everyone has demons to face, but your needs are never less important than those of anyone else.

Acknowledge what you need in a situation and be patient with yourself, even if nobody else seems to be. Recognize that you can't choose what feelings you have about a given situation. You can only choose what you do with those feelings. Set boundaries to protect yourself, and use affirmations to remind yourself that your well-being is important and that it's okay for you to go at your own pace. Choosing to take your time and protect yourself as you sort through emotions is a demonstration of good self-care.

"I broke up with my girlfriend again last week and am having a hard time moving on. I thought this time would be easier, but part of me misses her, even though I know she's not right for me. We've gotten back together so many times, but nothing really changes and every time we fight, I feel worse about myself. How do I stay strong with my decision to end things?"

Breaking up is never easy. Even if you 100% know it's not the right relationship for you, it's still so easy to get sucked back in. The thing about a breakup is that you not only lose your boyfriend or girlfriend, you also lose a best friend who you talked to every day and were excited to share all your news with. It's easy to miss this comfort and familiarity, which is why people often decide to stay friends. But the problem is that it's really hard to reestablish boundaries when you go from being in a relationship to being "just friends" without some space and time in between. It's just so easy to hook up "one last time," and it's hard not to get jealous if your ex starts dating somebody new.

The best remedy for a breakup really is time and distance. You need time to get comfortable being alone and to learn to be your own support person. At first, distance can make us forget the bad stuff as we miss and remember the good. If you find this happening, take out a piece of paper and draw a red flag on top. Then begin keeping a list of all the negatives in the relationship. Jot down any flaws in the other person, fights you recall, breaches of trust, and moments you doubted whether you were meant to be. When you miss the ex or find yourself on a slippery slope of being sucked back in, take a look at this list of red flags and remind yourself of the reasons you ended it in the first place. It's also useful to make a list of all the things you *do* want in a partner. How does your ex compare to this list? Chances are, they do not. Remember that it's hard to build self-esteem or be open to meeting somebody who is a better fit if you're stuck hanging on to a past relationship.

The Stairway to Healing

I like to use a staircase analogy to help maintain distance from an ex. Imagine that the breakup—and how terrible you are feeling now—is at the bottom of a staircase, and healing and moving on is at the top. Every day you refrain from interacting with your ex is like taking a step up. It's something you can feel proud of. But hanging out and having conversations before you've both moved on isn't just like a step down—it's like falling *all the way* back to the bottom. If you can focus on the end goal of healing, it's easier to see each day apart as an important part of you moving forward.

If your ex is not respecting your need for space or keeps popping up in your social media feed, you might want to block or mute them for a period of time. I find that it's best to let them know to avoid drama and hurt feelings. Say something like, "Hey, I want to let you know I'm going to mute you on social media for a while. It's not to be mean. It's just that I'm having a hard time moving on, and I think some distance will be best for us both." Creating distance can be hard in high school—especially if you attend the same school, are in the same classes, and share a friend group. But do your best to limit your interactions with an ex. Keep them brief and cordial, and you will feel stronger and more confident in your decision to move forward.

"For years I have been feeling really down. I have so much anxiety about everything, but nobody seems to understand. I manage to get good grades, so my parents always reassure me that I will be fine. But I can't stop focusing on the things that go wrong. If I get a 95% on a test, I beat myself up for the questions I got wrong. Even if we win our basketball games, I am still pissed at myself for the shots I missed. When I have plans with friends, I worry about how things will go. Then I constantly replay the night, getting upset with myself for anything stupid I said or did. The feelings of self-hatred have become so bad that I sometimes wish I weren't here at all."

This illustrates a classic case of low self-esteem fueled by negative self-talk. The key to getting unstuck will be to learn to stop mentally beating yourself up by changing your self-talk and instead using positive affirmations in how you think. Refer back to the exercises on pages 34 to 43. A lot of teens (and adults!) get trapped in a habit of self-destructive thinking, which can make life feel unbearable. What makes it worse is that these feelings and struggles are internal, so you likely feel really alone. To the outside world, you may look fine—you get good grades, are successful, have friends, and are loved by teachers. Nobody can really see or understand how terrible you feel on the inside.

If you're stuck feeling this way or have thoughts that things would be better if you weren't around, consider telling a parent you'd like to get some professional help in order to improve self-esteem and feel more optimistic about your future. Look for a cognitive behavioral therapy (CBT) or EMDR therapist. If your parents aren't motivated to find help, talk to your school counselor who can advocate for you and provide referrals to point you in the right direction. With help, you can change the patterns that are making you feel bad and rewire the way you think.

"A few years ago I got involved in a relationship online. At first, he was really nice, telling me I was attractive and really cool. We chatted every day and were interested in all the same things. But eventually, he started asking me to send nude photos and do things on video chat that made me uncomfortable. I didn't want him to think I was a loser, so I agreed. Turns out he was much older than me. Now I can't stop feeling dirty and damaged, and I'm freaked out by the fact that these pictures of me are out there. I can't believe I did these things."

First of all, I want anyone in a situation like this to understand this is absolutely not your fault and not something to be ashamed of. One of the very unfortunate realities of the world we live in is that it is filled with abusive people who prey on others. If you have ever been involved in a scenario where somebody has drawn you in, gained your trust and affection (a technique called "grooming"), then ultimately asked you to do things of a sexual nature (whether in person or virtually), you are a victim of sexual abuse, and it is never your fault.

No matter how agreeable or willing you may have been, your participation was a consequence of sexual abuse, which is a crime in our country and always the fault of the adult perpetrator who should have known better. In instances where sexual abuse occurs between two minors, there is likely a pedophile or another abuser who taught the other victim how to abuse, and they are ultimately responsible for the havoc that has trickled down to impact multiple lives.

If you are a victim of sexual abuse, please talk to an adult you can trust to get assistance in determining whether to report what happened and get support. Sexual abuse destroys self-esteem, and your best course of action will be to get into therapy where you can process what happened and heal. Please see the resources section at the end of this book.

"Lately I haven't been sleeping well at all! I toss and turn when trying to fall asleep, and sometimes I wake up in the middle of the night in a panic. I often have dreams that I forgot to do my homework. If I have a test or a game the next day, I wake my parents up, freaking out that I'm not prepared. They're frustrated with me and don't know how to help. They just keep reassuring me that I'm doing fine, but they don't understand I don't feel fine at all!"

When people become overwhelmed and feel out of control due to anxiety and incessant worry about every little thing, sleep can be impacted—and lack of sleep can make things feel even worse by creating a vicious cycle. When you have a lot on your plate and are constantly engaged in anxious self-talk like "What if I fail?" or "What if I'm not prepared?" or "What if I'm not ready for the game?" you wind up working yourself up, which makes everything feel overwhelming.

In these instances, it's helpful to take a step back and break down everything you have going on. Making a list can help. Think back to the stressors exercises on pages 79 to 81. When you get a clear picture of everything weighing on your mind—stress about a test, three chapters to read for English, soccer practice after school—it becomes easier to look at each individual item and think of the steps you need to take to feel okay. Rather than get stuck in feelings of being overwhelmed, you can put your energy into making a plan to tackle things. Be sure to use rational, calm self-talk. It might look something like this:

"I feel really overwhelmed. I have homework and a test to study for, and I also have soccer practice and need to feel ready for my game this weekend. I have to make it through the rest of the school day. All I can do between now and then is focus during my classes so I don't feel further behind. After school, I'll read as much as I can before soccer. At soccer I will stay focused and work on what I need to do for this weekend's games. After that, I'll finish the rest of the chapters, then move on to studying for the test. There's a lot on my plate tonight but I will be okay. If I stay calm and focused, I'll get through it. All that matters is I do the best I can."

Container Visualization/Meditation

If anxious self-talk around stressors is keeping you up at night, try this exercise:

Close your eyes and imagine a container with a lid. Now imagine it being large enough to contain all your stressors, anxieties, worries, tensions, and fears. Then imagine all those things going into the container, one by one.

When every last stressor is in there, imagine closing the lid and putting the container somewhere where you can store it—somewhere out of sight but easily accessible later. You can return to the container when you have the time, energy, and resources available to tackle what's inside. Think about how it feels to imagine having the power to contain your stressors.

Write a description of your container:

_____

_____

_____

Where did you store it?

_____

_____

_____

Use this exercise whenever you feel overwhelmed. The more you practice it, the better you will become at gaining some distance and perspective when life feels overwhelming.

"My boyfriend keeps pressuring me to have sex with him, but I'm not sure I'm ready. I'm afraid if I keep saying 'no,' he'll break up with me and tell everyone the reason why. Should I stop worrying and just do it?"

The teen years bring about lots of pressure when it comes to new experiences, especially sexually, but you should never feel pressured to comply just to please somebody else. Making decisions based on pleasing others at the expense of your own needs, wants, or values wreaks havoc on self-esteem and can lead to years of regret. If a partner is pressuring you in any way, take a step back and think about how your self-esteem is impacted by being in a relationship with somebody who doesn't respect your needs.

When you have healthy self-esteem, you aren't afraid of losing people due to standing up for yourself. If others do walk away, you are able to say "good riddance" and know you are better off alone than being with somebody who doesn't respect or deserve you. Think about this: If he doesn't respect you now, he probably won't respect you in the future. Would you rather be dumped by someone before or after you have sex with them? The right partner and person to choose to have sex with is somebody who cares about you enough to wait for you to be ready and comfortable. When you say "no" to somebody else, you say "yes" to taking care of yourself, and that builds self-esteem.

Review the exercises on people-pleasing (pages 57 and 58) and assertiveness (pages 82 to 87), and see if you can come up with an assertive message that will convey to your boyfriend that you are not ready, so he should stop asking, and that you will tell him if and when you change your mind. If he does break up with you or share your personal conversations with anyone, be prepared to stand up for yourself again, telling others that you wish they'd stay out of your personal life and respect that you have a right to decide for yourself about when—and with whom—you have sex.

"A bunch of my friends have started smoking pot after school, and they have been inviting me to join. I know someone who lost their ride to college after being kicked off the team for drug use. I don't want to risk it, but my friends won't stop nagging me to join. I'm afraid if I keep making excuses, they'll stop hanging out with me and think I'm totally lame. What should I do?"

Peer pressure around drinking and/or drugs is often a part of the high school experience, and it's really hard to weigh the potential future consequences of alcohol or drugs—getting caught, messing up your plans, becoming addicted, facing health issues—against the fear of having friends make fun of you if you say "no." Having just attended my 20-year high school reunion, there's one thing I can tell you for sure: Your health and future are *way* more important than the opinions of people you may drift apart from after you graduate.

As an adult, I'm probably supposed to tell you drugs are bad and you should stay away from people who do them. But that rigid direction doesn't help you make truly informed decisions nor learn to trust your own instincts. The important thing is that you make your own choices from a place of confidence, being informed, and using your own best judgment, not from peer pressure or the fear of being ridiculed or losing friends.

Use assertiveness skills to stand behind your decisions. There's nothing wrong with telling friends, "Thanks for the offer, but I'm not getting into it." If others don't accept your decision to decline something you aren't comfortable with, know that it's more about their issues than it is about you. It's perfectly fine to be friends with and hang out with people who make decisions that conflict with your own as long as you remain comfortable and safe doing so. But remember, if friends judge you and harass you for your choices, you may want to reconsider how authentic the friendships truly are.

If you choose to experiment with drugs and alcohol, do so with caution, knowing that you never fully know what is in a drug or unsealed drink—or how your body and mind will be affected. Be smart and know that drugs and alcohol can be highly addictive and lead you down a path you may regret. Advising teens to stay away from marijuana in particular is rather hard to do when so many states are starting to legalize it due to documented therapeutic and medicinal benefits. But the fact is, regular use of marijuana *does* impact the brain, damaging regions that control memory and learning. Potential impairment to a teen's brain is especially scary, considering that the human brain isn't even fully developed until around age 27. Before you decide whether and how often to use drugs, recognize that they have a real impact, and be careful not to form a habit that can pose a threat to your success.

"Last night we had family in town and were out to dinner until pretty late. I got most of my homework done, but by 1 a.m. I was exhausted and couldn't finish the paper due fifth period. I've never had a late assignment and don't know what to do. There's no way I can get it done, and I'm afraid my teacher will hate me."

As a teen, school is likely your main job and priority, but you are also human and sometimes life gets in the way. The best thing you can do in a situation where you can't honor a responsibility is be proactive in confronting the problem. Holding yourself accountable and admitting to something you don't feel great about may seem really challenging when self-esteem is low and you have trouble advocating for yourself. But remember that everyone has times where things don't go according to plan. Sometimes we all need to ask for a pass because we don't feel well, have an unexpected crisis, or just can't manage everything on the to-do list. It's part of being human.

When you fail to meet a deadline or can't fulfill an obligation, don't be afraid to own it with a sincere confession and apology if necessary. Most people will be understanding and forgiving, especially if it's unusual for you to not meet your responsibilities. Of course, there will always be some people who are overly strict or just not very sympathetic—some teachers don't seem to get that students have a life outside of their classes. But if you truly gave your best effort, other people's lack of understanding is likely more about them than it is about you. In either case, recognize that the situation is not the end of the world and move forward knowing you did the best you could. Being honest and upfront is something you can feel good about. When you tell yourself you did your best and handled things in the most mature way possible, you build self-esteem.

"I was really looking forward to the beach trip coming up, but now I'm dreading it. I was hoping to get in better shape, but I've been so busy I haven't had time to exercise. To make matters worse, my face just totally broke out. I hate that I'll be the ugly, fat one in all our pictures and everyone else will be all cute in their bikinis. Maybe if I skip every meal between now and Saturday I can at least lose a few pounds."

It's an awful feeling when you were looking forward to something only to have it approach and discover you aren't feeling great about yourself. But try your best to put aside your insecurities so you can have a good time. Remember that someone who is imperfect but confident is way more attractive than somebody who seems perfect but exudes insecurity. Nobody likes to be around people who constantly put themselves down or complain about things they really can't control.

Don't waste your energy trying fad diets or starving yourself. It only leads to "hangri-ness" and goes completely against the concepts of good self-care and self-compassion. Eat healthily because you want to be healthy and feel good. Then put on your cutest swimsuit and stand confidently. Body language goes a long way in increasing your level of attractiveness, so even if you don't feel great about yourself in the moment, fake it to the best of your ability by using affirmations like, "I'm okay, and I allow myself to have fun." Remember to put your shoulders back, stand up tall, and smile. People will be attracted to your confidence. Know that anyone who criticizes your appearance is likely trying to compensate for their own insecurities.

"It's been three weeks since I broke up with my boyfriend, and I thought I was finally moving on, but then I saw him at a fast food place last week. We ended up talking in his car for a while. He apologized for the mean stuff he said and told me he missed me. We've been talking and hanging out again and things were great at first, but last night we got in a fight, and he shoved me and threatened to smash my phone. I don't know what to do. Every time I think I've finally had it and decide to move on, he ends up being super sweet again, but it just never seems to last."

This sounds like the classic cycle in an abusive relationship, and I am going to be very blunt in telling you that abusive people *do not* change without serious help in the form of therapy and anger management education. Unfortunately, the majority of abusive people are not willing to get the help they need.

The cycle of abuse goes something like this: There is a period of time where things seem okay. The relationship may be going well, your partner may be treating you great, and you have a lot of fun together. But under the surface, tension is building. Little arguments occur and the abusive partner slowly starts doing things to hurt your feelings, isolate you from friends, and chip away at your self-esteem by making you doubt your worth. Eventually a blowup happens where the abuser attacks verbally and sometimes physically. (Know that there doesn't have to be physical violence for it to be abuse. Emotional abuse is every bit as damaging.) This explosive period is usually followed by the abusive partner apologizing profusely or making excuses about how their behavior was somehow your fault. Things go back to being okay for a while, but the cycle continues. Over time, the "good periods" become fewer and further between and the nature of the abuse gets worse.

Take a look at the following wheel to see if any of these behaviors apply to your relationship. Sometimes, it can be eye opening to recognize the various, subtle ways you are experiencing abuse.

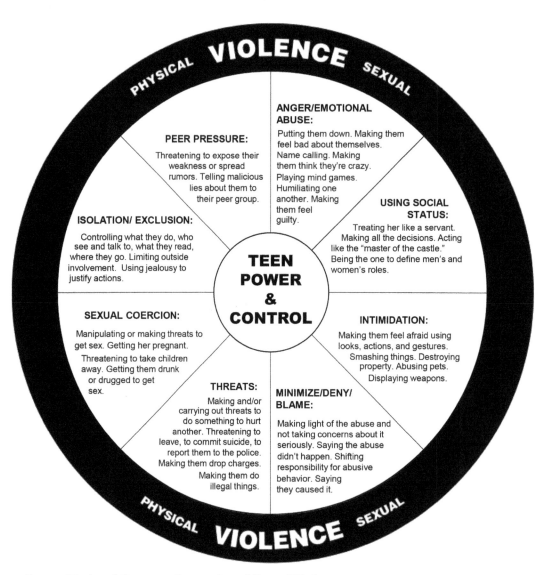

Source: National Center on Domestic and Sexual Violence

You will see that abusive behaviors center around a need for power and control. This makes it impossible to have the equality and respect that are necessary for a relationship to be healthy. Now take a look at the equality wheel and know that this is the type of relationship you deserve:

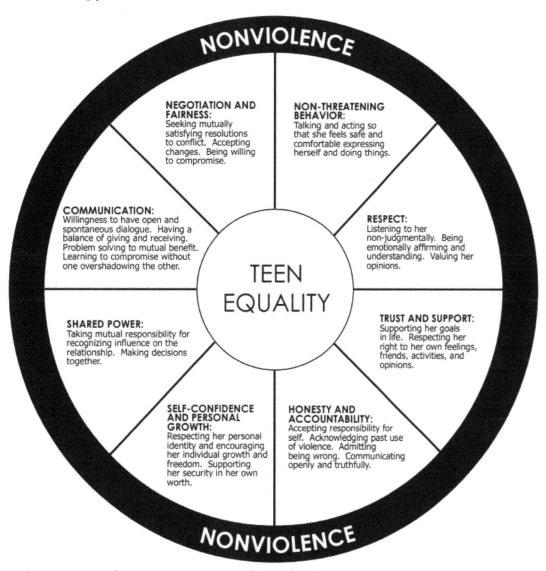

Source: National Center on Domestic and Sexual Violence

If you are in an abusive relationship, your self-esteem is being destroyed, and you need to get out. See the resources at the end of this book for help and make sure you can get support in staying safe when you end things.

Stages of Grief

It's not easy to walk away from a relationship, even one that is unhealthy. Breaking up involves a period of grieving, and you will likely have moments where you question your decision. It's normal to miss the good aspects of the relationship and the person you *wanted* your partner to be. Know that it will be a process that will likely include the following stages:

1. Denial: You are in shock and don't want to face the loss.
2. Anger: You become angry at various people, the situation, or the world.
3. Bargaining: You get caught up in fantasies that often begin with "If only . . . "
4. Depression: You feel utterly sad and alone and fear things will never get better.
5. Acceptance: You begin to come to terms with the loss. Eventually, you will feel at peace with it.

Everybody's grief process is different, and we don't necessarily go through these stages in a nice, neat order. You may find yourself cycling back and forth between these emotions, so be patient as you allow yourself to experience each emotion and trust that, with time, you will feel better.

"Last week, my parents walked in on me passing a Juul with my friends. They freaked out and since then have been lecturing me at every opportunity. My mom is really upset because my grandfather died of lung cancer. But e-cigs aren't the same as smoking! I don't know why they don't get that. How can I make them understand that vaping is safe and everybody does it?"

I have to admit that when I learned about all the different flavors Juul offers, it did sound pretty appealing! Vape pens in general are pretty cool in theory—they offer a discreet way to get a buzz and eliminate the smell (and risks) of second-hand smoke. But even though they were invented to offer a safer alternative for smokers who wanted to smoke less or ultimately quit, vaping has led to an increase in nicotine addiction, especially in the teen population. Between 2017 and 2018, there was a 75% increase in e-cigarette use among high school students. That's a pretty big increase, and I can't help but wonder if they will still be as popular in the future once we know more about their long-term effects.

Some studies indicate that health risks include a 71% increased risk of stroke, 59% increased risk of heart attack, and 40% increased risk of heart disease. Those are some pretty high percentages. Vaping is also reported to create psychiatric problems, including addiction, anxiety, a lack of focus, and interference in brain development. It can also cause headaches and stomachaches.

Can you believe that only a few decades ago people could smoke cigarettes on airplanes and inside of restaurants and offices? Those concepts seem so foreign to many of us now, but cigarette smoking was huge—until we discovered how harmful it really is. E-cigarettes are supposed to be a healthier alternative, but critics warn that one Juul cartridge contains the same amount of nicotine as a *pack* of cigarettes and that you can't know what chemicals are actually in the oils you are vaping unless you have them tested in a lab.

We know that nicotine, in any form, is a chemical that changes the brain—and there is concern that a developing teen brain may be more vulnerable to the addictive effects. Given all these risk factors, it makes sense that parents would be concerned and disapprove of vaping. Teens need to be informed of the negative consequences of vaping and realize it may not be as safe as you think. Scientists are still studying the long-term effects of e-cigarettes, and you need to consider whether you want to be a guinea pig in that research. Although vaping may seem to be the cool thing to do now, is it worth risking your future health? If you decide it's not something you want to engage in, find the courage to skip your hit and remain confident in your decision, even when others don't share your same hesitation.

"I'm finally coming to terms with the fact that I'm gay, but the past few years have been really rough. When my friend found out I had a crush on them, they got freaked out, so I pretended it was just a joke and then hooked up with a few members of the opposite sex to try to prove I was straight. But it backfired and rumors went around that I was a slut. Now I like somebody in one of my classes, but I'm afraid they will reject me because of the rumors. What should I do?"

My heart goes out to anyone who gets bullied or suffers as the victim of unkind rumors or gossip. It's a sad truth that kids will sometimes encounter peers who are just plain cruel, and, unfortunately, our world of technology allows the meanness to thrive through cyberbullying and slut-shaming via social media. Bullying destroys self-esteem and creates feelings of isolation and humiliation. Remember that anyone who bullies usually does so because they feel inadequate. They have the false belief that shifting the focus to somebody else will help them feel better. Feeling empathy for bullies and seeing them as sad and lost can help you feel empowered and allow you to rise above the havoc they create.

Exploring sexually and figuring out your sexuality can be a complex endeavor, especially when you feel the whole school knows your private business. Coming out can also be a major challenge given the stigma that still remains around homosexuality in our society. There's so much fear of being rejected, and it makes sense that LGBTQ teens may initially try to deny or hide their true identities. It's important to recognize that coming to terms with who you are as a sexual being is a journey, and if you do identify as LGBTQ, coming out may take time. The process will look different for each individual, and each person will face varying levels of acceptance from their family, friends, and social network.

If you've struggled with accepting who you are, remember that your worth as a human is not dependent on how you identify, how others treat you, or what other people choose to think or believe. Your value cannot be impacted by the ignorance, close-mindedness, or biases of others unless you allow your own negative self-talk to make you feel ashamed. Use affirmations that help you feel proud of who you are. Try your best to ignore or assertively confront the mean-spirited comments and actions of others. The more you own and celebrate who you are, the easier it will become to feel confident in speaking your truth and defending yourself against any discrimination you may face.

Recognize that mistakes are a natural part of life and are how we learn and grow. You may have regrets regarding past hookups or what others know about you, and it may feel like you can never get past the feelings of shame and humiliation. But be patient and kind to yourself. In the long run, you will move beyond this period, and the people who are truly worthy of your time and affection will accept you for who you are. We all have some level of baggage at some point in our lives, but your ability to forgive yourself and move forward will be a trait worthy of admiration.

"I had a lot on my mind during tonight's basketball game and ended up missing an important free throw. Because of it, we lost the game, and I know everyone was bummed. I'm afraid to face my teammates and coach again. I'm thinking of just quitting and never going back."

Running away and hiding often seems a lot more appealing than dealing with confrontation or facing the disappointment of others head-on. But remember that you are human! Everyone makes mistakes, and this setback is *not* the end of the world. Trust me—you are ruminating on your mistake *way* more than anyone else, and in the grand scheme of things, losing this one game won't hugely impact the course of your life. Quitting the team, however, may create lasting feelings of shame and regret.

When we give up on something for the wrong reasons—like being driven by fear rather than a legitimate desire to quit—we create bigger problems that impact self-esteem. Allowing embarrassment and fear of judgment to control you ruins confidence and holds you back. Acknowledge to yourself and your teammates that you are disappointed and really wish things had turned out differently, then move on, using positive affirmations such as, "This too shall pass" and "Everyone makes mistakes." Your ability to face this setback with grace and strength is every bit as impressive as if you had made that basket.

"I feel so overwhelmed. I'm taking mostly advanced placement classes, am involved in two clubs and a sport, and also agreed to help my friend on the planning committee for the winter dance. My parents are on my case about my college applications, but at the end of the day, I'm exhausted and keep putting them off. I want my college application to be strong and want to go somewhere good, but I'm so stressed and not sure I can handle it all. How do I manage?"

The pressure to get into a good college is huge during high school. It's true that college is important since many occupations now require an advanced degree, but getting into a specific university doesn't define you and where you end up going doesn't necessarily make or break your future. Achieving a college degree does open doors, increases career opportunities, and improves your chances of success. But just as important as this piece of paper are qualities like motivation, determination, a good work ethic, and being realistic with how much you can juggle.

Overscheduling yourself to the point of exhaustion puts you at risk for burning out. Rather than overwhelm yourself with a bunch of honors classes and a ton of extracurricular activities, set realistic goals and focus on the things that are most important to you. Recognize that saying "no" or dropping certain classes doesn't need to be viewed as a failure. Putting your energy into doing your best in a few areas and setting boundaries regarding how much you can take on are accomplishments and important parts of self-care. Watch out for perfectionist tendencies that make you believe you have to do everything. Use healthy self-talk around keeping yourself focused and stable, and then break your responsibilities down into small steps that feel manageable.

COLLEGE APPLICATION CHECKLIST

When it comes to applying for colleges, the following chart can help you get started. By organizing your options and having a clear picture of what's on your to-do list, you can more easily tackle those applications and feel good about the progress you are making. Remember to use positive self-talk and give yourself praise for even the smallest accomplishments.

COLLEGE	APPLICATION DEADLINE	EARLY DEADLINE	COMMON APP	TO DO
			☐ Yes ☐ No	☐ Application completed ☐ Transcript sent ☐ Test scores sent ☐ Recommendation letters sent ☐ Essay(s) sent ☐ Application fee paid
			☐ Yes ☐ No	☐ Application completed ☐ Transcript sent ☐ Test scores sent ☐ Recommendation letters sent ☐ Essay(s) sent ☐ Application fee paid
			☐ Yes ☐ No	☐ Application completed ☐ Transcript sent ☐ Test scores sent ☐ Recommendation letters sent ☐ Essay(s) sent ☐ Application fee paid

COLLEGE	APPLICATION DEADLINE	EARLY DEADLINE	COMMON APP	TO DO
			☐ Yes ☐ No	☐ Application completed ☐ Transcript sent ☐ Test scores sent ☐ Recommendation letters sent ☐ Essay(s) sent ☐ Application fee paid
			☐ Yes ☐ No	☐ Application completed ☐ Transcript sent ☐ Test scores sent ☐ Recommendation letters sent ☐ Essay(s) sent ☐ Application fee paid
			☐ Yes ☐ No	☐ Application completed ☐ Transcript sent ☐ Test scores sent ☐ Recommendation letters sent ☐ Essay(s) sent ☐ Application fee paid
			☐ Yes ☐ No	☐ Application completed ☐ Transcript sent ☐ Test scores sent ☐ Recommendation letters sent ☐ Essay(s) sent ☐ Application fee paid

Remember that choosing which college you will attend is an important decision, but it's not one that has to define your future. Know that nothing is set in stone. Don't let the process and the ultimate decision regarding where you go to college overwhelm you. There are many paths to success, and the direction of your future may change course many times throughout your life. There are always options available, including taking a gap year, transferring schools, changing majors, and pursuing advanced degrees later in life. Set realistic expectations for yourself so you can enjoy your high school experience without regret rather than be overwhelmed by it.

"It's starting to get warmer out, and I'm nervous about wearing shorts and short sleeves. Last fall, I started self-harming, and now I feel self-conscious about the scars on my arms and legs. Somebody in class already noticed marks and asked what happened. I said I fell into a thorny bush, but I felt weird about lying and don't know if it's believable. What should I do?"

Scars and discomfort around how to explain them is a very real consequence of cutting, but one that often goes ignored during times of stress when people feel they have no other coping skills to turn to. Refer back to the coping skills exercises on pages 88 to 90. There are lots of other ways to deal with stress. It may take some trial and error to find out what works best for you, but strive to use healthy coping tools rather than self-harm.

If you've already begun self-harming to cope, it can be difficult to stop. But set a goal

at least one or two things from your coping skills box *before* you turn to self-harm.

ften occurs when somebody has passed the point of thinking rationally, so work

rapist who can help you pinpoint your triggers and learn to utilize coping skills

stress escalates to the point of no return.

not a lot you can do about previous wounds aside from applying scar-removal

giving them time to heal. And there's no single answer regarding how to

tions from others. But cutting often persists when the secrecy around it

lthough you don't have to tell everybody the truth about your scars, consider

ir struggles with people you can trust. Opening up can help you gain

gin to heal. See the resources section for help finding a therapist.

"I'm working to build self-esteem, but I feel like it's one step forward, two steps back because people's criticisms really get to me. Lately my friends have been on my case about talking to this new kid I met at a party, and my parents keep jumping down my throat about needing to be more helpful around the house. Yesterday my English teacher handed back my first draft and the entire paper was covered in red ink. Today my coach kept me after practice to talk about what I need to work on. How can I feel good about myself when everybody seems to think I am doing everything wrong?"

When self-esteem is low, any critique—whether constructive or destructive, founded or unfounded—feels like an attack and can make us ruminate on the fact that we feel like we suck. But remember that how you feel isn't really about the criticism or the opinion of the critic—it's about how *you think* about the criticism. When we think in negative, self-deprecating ways, we wind up fixating on the criticism and allow it to destroy our self-esteem. We tell ourselves that because someone insinuated that we were bad or wrong, we must be bad or wrong in general. When we can see the criticism from a broader perspective and consider alternatives that don't relate to our worth, we can think more rationally. By taking a step back and evaluating the intent and validity of a criticism, we can protect our self-esteem.

To illustrate this concept, consider two different ways of thinking about the feedback from each person:

* Friends:
  * Negative self-talk: *My friends think I'm a loser with terrible taste. I can't trust my own opinions.*
  * Positive self-talk: *Maybe my friends are just jealous. Or maybe they have reason to dislike this person and want to protect me because I matter to them.*

* Parents:
  * Negative self-talk: *My parents think I'm a lazy slob.*
  * Positive self-talk: *My parents are tired after work. They count on me to help out.*

* English teacher:
  * Negative self-talk: *My teacher hated everything I wrote! I suck at English.*
  * Positive self-talk: *My teacher put a lot of effort into making suggestions that will help me improve my writing. Maybe she wants to help me because she sees my potential.*

* Coach:
  * Negative self-talk: *My coach thinks I'm terrible. Clearly I'm the worst player on the team.*
  * Positive self-talk: *My coach likes me and is taking a special interest in helping me fine-tune my skills because he knows I can be really good.*

When self-esteem is low, we accept criticism at face value and allow it to confirm feelings of self-doubt and unworthiness. To build self-esteem, you must begin looking at criticism through a different, more open-minded lens. Rather than let criticism reinforce low self-esteem, take a step back and think about what the criticism really means. What is the intent of the critic? Are they meaning to shame and embarrass you? Do they want you to change to better meet their needs? Are they somehow concerned about you? Or do they want to help you grow in some way?

When you stop to consider the intent, validity, and the bigger picture surrounding a criticism, you protect self-esteem by establishing that criticism doesn't necessarily suggest or confirm a personal flaw. When criticism is destructive, recognize that it may be more about the other person than it is about you. Do your best to either confront it assertively or ignore it and move on. When criticism is constructive, see it as an opportunity to learn and grow. Either way, use positive self-talk to remind yourself that mistakes are how we learn and that you are human.

"My parents are going through a divorce, and it's been really rough. They are always in bad moods and life feels miserable. My mom and I always fight and sometimes she yells, "You're just like your father." Rationally, I know their splitting up is not my fault, but sometimes I wonder if I'm the reason their marriage didn't work out. Will things ever be okay again?"

Separation and divorce can be a really difficult time for everyone in a family, and kids often internalize the stress and question whether they played a role in contributing to their parents' troubles. Divorce is *never* a kid's fault, but they often become a casualty as parents stumble over how to handle their own anger and grief. As you are watching the chaos unfold, you likely recognize that your parents have flaws and are *not* perfect. If you can develop an appreciation for the fact that your parents are imperfect humans struggling with their own emotions, you can better separate yourself from self-blame and protect your self-esteem.

It can be really hard to feel good about yourself when a parent is accusing you of being just like the person they are divorcing, but know that is just the anger and stress talking. You have qualities of *both* parents, and as you are becoming more mature and independent, you can make choices regarding which of their positive qualities you want to claim versus which of their flaws you can learn from and disown.

As you navigate the stress of divorce, try not to bottle up your feelings. Talk to a friend, school counselor, or therapist about what you are going through. Use assertiveness skills and set boundaries with your parents. It's okay to respectfully tell them you don't appreciate their taking the stress out on you. Standing up for yourself will help you protect your self-esteem and prevent it from being negatively impacted by the divorce. See the resources section for books that can help your family during this time.

"I was born with a heart condition and can't participate in many physical activities, like playing sports. I don't attend school dances and events because I don't want to be the person awkwardly standing alone on the sidelines. As I've gotten older, people have started to notice that I am different, and most people just ignore me. Others seem to resent that I don't have to take gym class and that teachers excuse my absences due to frequent doctor appointments. In classes, I've noticed people staring and whispering about me, and I don't know what to do. How do I make friends when I feel so different and people don't seem to understand me?"

Anyone with an uncommon disorder or rare condition faces challenges when it comes to fitting in and figuring out how to explain their situation to others. An unfortunate reality in our society seems to be that ignorance and a lack of understanding regarding differences often lead to avoidance—and sometimes even bullying.

I encourage you to embrace your uniqueness and find the courage to educate people about your condition. Often people avoid those who are different due to fear of offending or saying the wrong thing. This is about them and not you. By addressing the elephant in the room and letting others know that you are open to sharing information about your condition, you break the ice and give others the opportunity to get to know you and learn more about your experience.

One of the most inspiring people I've worked with is a college student who lost his hand in an accident. The attitude with which he faced the ordeal was incredible. Although some people would get stuck in a place of depression, regret, and self-pity, he moved forward with a strong conviction that he could rise above the tragedy, get back to doing everything he once did, and could ultimately inspire others by sharing how amazing bionic hand technology is. By owning your difference and choosing to see yourself as unique rather than odd or shameful, you can face the world with a sense of courage and confidence that will be inspiring and attractive to others.

YOU'RE ON YOUR WAY

After spending time working through the exercises in this book and learning new skills, you'll hopefully be well on the path to improving your self-esteem. You might also be caught up in sorting through the various experiences and challenges that led to issues with low self-esteem—and that's okay. Remember that everybody's experience with building self-esteem will be unique. Part of healthy self-care involves treating yourself with patience and having self-compassion as you strive to make improvements and find self-acceptance. Diving into issues around self-esteem struggles can sometimes open up cans of worms that require us to spend time exploring and healing wounds from the past. Often, things may feel worse before better. But take your time and trust that developing healthy self-esteem will happen as you continue to put these tools into practice.

Once your self-esteem is in an optimal place, maintaining it will be a lifelong journey. It will be important to keep all these skills and tools in mind and use them throughout your life. Sometimes, things seem better and then life throws us a curveball that derails our progress and results in our reverting back to old, unhealthy patterns. Hang onto this book and set a goal to review some of the exercises every so often to see how you've grown and remind yourself of the tools and techniques you need to continue using to stay on track with healthy self-esteem. I promise that with practice and persistence, skills like healthy self-talk and assertiveness will become easier and feel more like second nature. Before we end, take a moment to plot where you feel your self-esteem is today.

LOW SELF-ESTEEM  HIGH SELF-ESTEEM

If there has been a positive change in your level of self-esteem from where you first started (page 28), give yourself credit for the hard work you've invested. If you still have a ways to go, don't worry! Building self-esteem takes time, and you have the rest of your life to keep improving. Continue to be realistic with your goals, and remember to be kind to yourself as you keep on moving forward.

Resources for Teens

To find more information and bonus material, visit www.meganmaccutcheon.com/teens.

Finding Help

SEARCH FOR THERAPISTS AND SUPPORT GROUPS

EMDRIA (Find an EMDR therapist)

www.emdria.org

Good Therapy

www.goodtherapy.org

Psychology Today

www.psychologytoday.com

National Alliance on Mental Illness

www.nami.org

Substance Abuse and Mental Health Services Administration

www.samhsa.gov

HELP HOTLINES

The National Domestic Violence Hotline

800-799-7233

National Suicide Prevention Lifeline

800-273-8255

National Sexual Assault Hotline

800-656-4673

HELP TEXTLINES

www.crisistextline.org/texting-in

Text "HOME" to 741-741

www.prsinc.org/crisislink/services/crisislink-hotlines

Text "CONNECT" to 85511

TREATMENT PROGRAMS

https://www.psychologytoday.com/us/treatment-rehab/teens-adolescent-residential

www.lindnercenterofhope.org/adolescents

Additional Information by Topic

ABUSE

National Center on Domestic and Sexual Violence

www.ncdsv.org

ADDICTION

Al-Anon Family Groups Teen Corner

www.al-anon.org/newcomers/teen-corner-alateen

Foote, Jeffrey, and Carrie Wilkens. *Beyond Addiction: How Science and Kindness Help People Change.* New York: Scribner, 2014.

Moderation Management™

www.moderation.org

ASSERTIVENESS TRAINING

Alberti, Robert E., and Michael L. Emmons. *Your Perfect Right: Assertiveness and Equality in your Life and Relationships.* 10th ed. Oakland, CA: Impact Publishers, 2017.

BODY IMAGE AND EATING ISSUES

Eating Disorder Hope

www.eatingdisorderhope.com

National Eating Disorders Association (NEDA)

www.nationaleatingdisorders.org

DIVORCE

Wallerstein, Judith S., Julia M. Lewis, and Sandra Blakeslee. *The Unexpected Legacy of Divorce: The 25 Year Landmark Study.* New York: Hyperion, 2000.

LGBTQ SUPPORT

Centers for Disease Control and Prevention: LGBT Youth Resources

https://www.cdc.gov/lgbthealth/youth-resources.htm

GLSEN

https://www.glsen.org

National Youth Advocacy Coalition
http://www.nyacyouth.org
PFLAG
https://pflag.org
The Trevor Project
www.thetrevorproject.org

MOOD DISORDERS

Bourne, Edmund J. *The Anxiety & Phobia Workbook*. 6th ed. Oakland, CA: New Harbinger Publications, 2015.

Ilardi, Stephen S. *The Depression Cure: The 6-Step Program to Beat Depression without Drugs*. Cambridge, MA: Da Capo Press, 2009.

SELF-CARE AND SELF-COMPASSION

Brown, Brené. *Daring Greatly: How the Courage to be Vulnerable Transforms the Way We Live, Love, Parent, and Lead*. New York: Gotham Books, 2012.

Brown, Brené. *The Gifts of Imperfection: Let Go of Who You Think You're Supposed to Be and Embrace Who You Are*. Center City, Minnesota: Hazelden, 2010.

Neff, Kristin. *Self-Compassion: The Proven Power of Being Kind to Yourself*. New York: Harper Collins, 2011.

SELF-INJURY

S.A.F.E. Alternatives
www.selfinjury.com

Shapiro, Lawrence E. *Stopping the Pain: A Workbook for Teens Who Cut and Self-Injure*. Oakland, CA: Instant Help, 2008.

SEXUAL ABUSE

Mather, Cynthia L. *How Long Does It Hurt? A Guide to Recovering from Incest and Sexual Abuse for Teenagers, Their Friends, and Their Families*. Plano, TX: Jossey-Bass, 2014.

National Center of Missing and Exploited Children: Report an Incident
http://www.missingkids.com/gethelpnow/cybertipline

SCIENCE

Arden, John B. *Rewire Your Brain: Think Your Way to a Better Life*. Hoboken, NJ: John Wiley & Sons, 2010.

Resources for Parents

Aha! Parenting

www.ahaparenting.com

Center for Parent/Youth Understanding

https://cpyu.org

Child Development Institute

https://childdevelopmentinfo.com/ages-stages/teenager-adolescent-development-parenting

Faber, Adele, and Elaine Mazlish. *How to Talk So Teens Will Listen and Listen So Teens Will Talk*. New York: HarperCollins, 2006.

Focus on the Family

www.focusonthefamily.com

HelpGuide

www.helpguide.org/home-pages/teen-issues.htm

KidsHealth

https://kidshealth.org/en/parents/adolescence.html

ParenTeen Connect

https://www.parenteenconnect.org

U.S. Department of Health and Human Services—Office of Population Affairs

www.hhs.gov/ash/oah/resources-and-training/for-families/index.html

Wallerstein, Judith S., and Sandra Blakeslee. *What About the Kids? Raising Your Children Before, During, and After Divorce*. New York: Hyperion, 2003.

REFERENCES

Alberti, Robert E., and Michael L. Emmons. *Your Perfect Right: Assertiveness and Equality in Your Life and Relationships*. 9th ed. Atascadero, CA: Impact Publishers, 2008.

Arden, John B. *Rewire Your Brain: Think Your Way to a Better Life*. Hoboken, NJ: John Wiley & Sons, 2010.

Bourne, Edmund J. *The Anxiety & Phobia Workbook*. 4th ed. Oakland, CA: New Harbinger Publications, 2005.

Bower, Sharon Anthony, and Gordon H. Bower. *Asserting Yourself: A Practical Guide for Positive Change*. Rev. ed. Cambridge, MA: Da Capo Press, 2004.

Branden, Nathaniel. *The Six Pillars of Self-Esteem: The Definitive Work on Self-Esteem by the Leading Pioneer in the Field*. New York: Bantam Books, 1995.

Brown, Brené. *Daring Greatly: How the Courage to Be Vulnerable Transforms the Way We Live, Love, Parent, and Lead*. New York: Gotham Books, 2012.

Brown, Brené. *I Thought It Was Just Me (But It Isn't): Making the Journey from "What Will People Think?" to "I Am Enough."* New York: Avery, 2007.

Brown, Brené. *The Gifts of Imperfection: Let Go of Who You Think You're Supposed to Be and Embrace Who You Are*. Center City, MN: Hazelden, 2010.

Burns, David D. *Feeling Good: The New Mood Therapy*. New York: HarperCollins, 1980.

Burns, David D. *Ten Days to Self-Esteem*. New York: HarperCollins, 1993.

Burns, David D. *The Feeling Good Handbook*. Rev ed. New York: Plume, 1999.

Clear Recovery Center. "What Drugs Can Be Smoked Out of an Electronic Cigarette." Accessed May 8, 2019. https://clearrecoverycenter.com/what-drugs-can-be -smoked-out-of-an-electronic-cigarette.

Domestic Abuse Intervention Programs: Home of The Duluth Model. www.theduluthmodel.org.

Engel, Beverly. *Loving Him Without Losing You: How to Stop Disappearing and Start Being Yourself.* New York: John Wiley & Sons, 2000.

Frankl, Viktor Emil. *Man's Search for Meaning.* Boston: Beacon Press, 2006.

Ganim, Sara, and Scott Zamost. "Vaping: The Latest Scourge in Drug Abuse." *CNN.* Last modified September 5, 2015. https://www.cnn.com/2015/09/04/us/ vaping-abuse/index.html.

Griffin, Eve, Elaine McMahon, Fiona McNicholas, Paul Corcoran, Ivan J. Perry, and Ella Arensman. "Increasing Rates of Self-Harm Among Children, Adolescents, and Young Adults: A 10-Year National Registry Study 2007–2016." *Social Psychiatry and Psychiatric Epidemiology* 53, no. 7 (2018): 663–671.

Hay, Louise L. *You Can Heal Your Life.* Carlsbad, CA: Hay House, 1999.

Johnson, Sharon L. *Therapist's Guide to Clinical Intervention: The 1-2-3's of Treatment Planning.* 2nd ed. San Diego, CA: Academic Press, 2004.

Kilbourne, Jean. *Killing Us Softly 4: Advertising's Image of Women.* Directed by Sut Jhally. Northampton, MA: Media Education Foundation, 2010.

MacCutcheon, Megan. *Building Self-Esteem: A Guide to Achieving Self-Acceptance & a Healthier, Happier, Life.* Washington, D.C.: Balancing Project Press, 2014.

MacCutcheon, Megan. *The Self-Esteem Workbook for Women: 5 Steps to Gaining Confidence and Inner Strength.* Emeryville, CA: Althea Press, 2018.

Maine, Margo. *Body Wars: Making Peace with Women's Bodies.* Carlsbad, CA: Gürze Books, 2000.

McGinley, Laurie. "FDA Chief Calls Youth E-Cigarettes an 'Epidemic.'" *The Washington Post*. September 12, 2018. https://www.washingtonpost.com/national/health-science /fda-chief-calls-youth-use-of-juul-other-e-cigarettes-an-epidemic/2018/09/12 /ddaa6612-b5c8-11e8-a7b5-adaaa5b2a57f_story.html?utm_term=.5995adb358de.

McQuaid, Michelle. "Wish You Could Banish Self-Doubt?" *Huffington Post*. Last modified June 26, 2015. https://www.huffingtonpost.com/michelle-mcquaid/ wish-you-could-banish-sel_b_7148754.html.

Miller, Korin, and Lyndsey Matthews. "What Is Juuling and Is it Really that Bad for Your Health?" *Women's Health*. Last modified September 12, 2018. https://www.womenshealthmag.com/health/a18377132/juuling.

National Center on Domestic and Sexual Violence. http://www.ncdsv.org.

Nedelman, Michael. "Why Vaping Is So Dangerous for Teens." *CNN*. Last modified January 17, 2019. https://www.cnn.com/2019/01/17/health/vaping-ecigarettes -kids-teens-brains-fda/index.html.

Neff, Kristin. *Self-Compassion: The Proven Power of Being Kind to Yourself.* New York: Harper Collins, 2011.

Oprah's Lifeclass. "Oprah and Dr. Brené Brown on Vulnerability and Daring Greatly." Season 3, Episode 314. OWN. September 22, 2013.

Peale, Norman Vincent. *The Power of Positive Thinking.* Rev. ed. New York: Fireside, 2007.

Roberts, Emily. "How Sleep Impacts Your Self-Esteem." *HealthyPlace.com*. April 4, 2014. https://www.healthyplace.com/blogs/buildingselfesteem/2014/04/how-sleep -impacts-your-self-esteem.

Russello, Salenna. "The Impact of Media Exposure on Self-Esteem and Body Satisfaction in Men and Women." *Journal of Interdisciplinary Undergraduate Research 1* (2009): Article 4. https://knowledge.e.southern.edu/jiur/vol1/iss1/4.

Schroll, Andrea V. "10 Things You Can Do Today to Overcome Self-Doubt." *Huffington Post*. Last modified April 28, 2017. https://www.huffingtonpost.com/andrea-v-schroll-/10-things-you-can-do-today-to-overcome-self-doubt_b_9777824.html.

Smith, Ann W. *Overcoming Perfectionism: Finding the Key to Balance and Self-Acceptance*. Rev. and updated. Deerfield Beach, FL: Health Communications, 2013.

Thompson, Dennis. "Vaping Tied to Rise in Stroke, Heart Attack Risk." *WebMD*. January 30, 2019. https://www.webmd.com/smoking-cessation/news/20190130/vaping-tied-to-rise-in-stroke-heart-attack-risk#1.

Tousignant, Lauren. "Now There's Proof Thin Models Ruin Your Self-Esteem." *New York Post*. August 30, 2017. https://nypost.com/2017/08/30/now-theres-proof-thin-models-ruin-your-self-esteem.

Tugend, Alina. "Praise is Fleeting, But Brickbats We Recall." *The New York Times*. March 23, 2012. http://www.nytimes.com/2012/03/24/your-money/why-people-remember-negative-events-more-than-positive-ones.html.

Warrell, Margie. "Is Self-Doubt Holding You Back? 5 Ways to Build Confidence and Banish Doubt." *Forbes*. September 18, 2014. https://www.forbes.com/sites/margiewarrell/2014/09/18/banish-doubt-build-confidence.

Whitfield, Charles L. *Boundaries and Relationships: Knowing, Protecting and Enjoying the Self*. Deerfield Beach, FL: Health Communications, 2010.

Wilding, Melody. "3 Ways Highly Successful People Handle Self Doubt." *Forbes*. April 5, 2017. https://www.forbes.com/sites/melodywilding/2017/04/05/3-ways-highly-successful-people-handle-self-doubt/#19a802e6789f.

Zenger, Jack, and Joseph Folkman. "The Ideal Praise-to-Criticism Ratio." *Harvard Business Review*. March 15, 2013. https://hbr.org/2013/03/the-ideal-praise-to-criticism.

INDEX

ABOUT THE AUTHOR

Megan MacCutcheon is a licensed professional counselor with a private practice in Vienna, Virginia. She specializes in working with individuals struggling with issues related to identity, self-esteem, trauma, depression, anxiety, and postpartum mood and anxiety disorders using CBT, EMDR, and mindfulness-based approaches. Megan received her Master of Education in community agency counseling from George Mason University and her Bachelor of Science in communication from Boston University. Megan is a self-esteem topic expert and contributor for the GoodTherapy.org blog.

Find additional resources and learn more about Megan at her website: MeganMacCutcheon.com.